SURVIVAL IN THE VALLEY OF DEATH
HOLOCAUST 1940–1945
Flory A. Van Beek

SEVEN LOCKS PRESS

Santa Ana, California
Minneapolis, Minnesota
Washington D.C.

Seven Locks Press
PO Box 25689
Santa Ana, CA 92799
(800) 354-5348

Book design by:
Sparrow Advertising & Design

Manufactured in the United States of America

Library of Congress Cataloging in Publication data is available
ISBN 0-929765-63-X

Dedication

I have written this testimonial in the sacred memory of my beloved mother and all family members who perished at the hands of the German Nazis in the greatest human tragedy the world has ever known.

In the Jewish faith it is an unbearable thought that the names of deceased ones have been blotted out without knowing where they perished and where they are buried.

It is my fervent wish that with this testimonial their blessed memories will live on through future generations, though their hopes and dreams were brutally destroyed.

This book will also serve as a tribute to the gracious people, total strangers, who gave us shelter in the most dangerous of circumstances. They have shown extraordinary courage and risked their own lives in the face of the enemy.

Newport Beach, California, USA, May 1998

Table of Contents

THE DEPORTATIONS

THE HIDING YEARS

THE LABYRINTH

WORKING FOR THE RESISTANCE

QUO VADIS?

THE YEAR OF RENEWED HOPE

MIRACLES DO HAPPEN

THE ROAD TO FREEDOM

THE END OF THE ROAD

Before I could finish my sentence there was an enormous explosion. Felix was thrown against the floor of the deck with such force that he could not get up. I also hit the deck floor with such velocity that I couldn't move. Children were screaming, water was gushing all over, and people were yelling and moaning. Someone from the crew yelled, "Up, up, we have to get up!" Shattered glass was all over the place. It was an apocalypse, a "Dante's Hell."

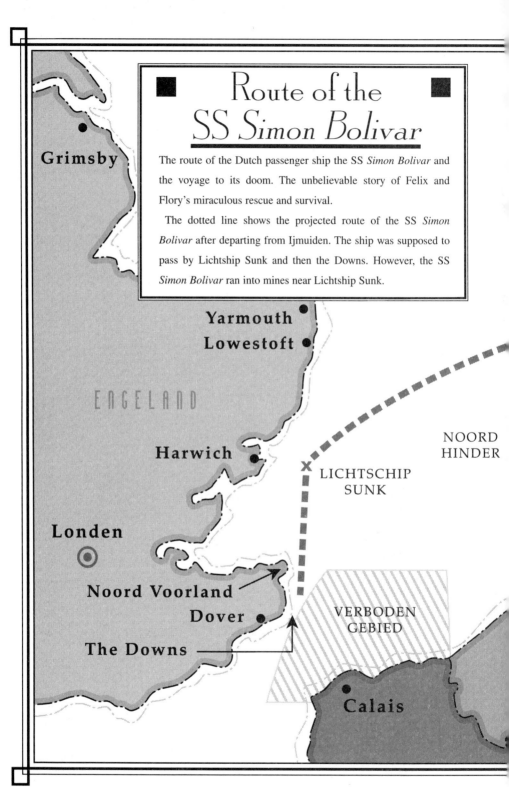

Route of the SS *Simon Bolivar*

The route of the Dutch passenger ship the SS *Simon Bolivar* and the voyage to its doom. The unbelievable story of Felix and Flory's miraculous rescue and survival.

The dotted line shows the projected route of the SS *Simon Bolivar* after departing from Ijmuiden. The ship was supposed to pass by Lichtship Sunk and then the Downs. However, the SS *Simon Bolivar* ran into mines near Lichtship Sunk.

Grimsby

Yarmouth
Lowestoft

ENGELAND

Harwich

NOORD HINDER

LICHTSCHIP SUNK

Londen

Noord Voorland

Dover

VERBODEN GEBIED

The Downs

Calais

My beloved mother

THE EARLY YEARS

Chapter 1: Amersfoort

"You can take your skates along with you today," I heard my mother say as I was preparing for school.

My family lived in a small town in the Netherlands, the country of my birth. The town was called Amersfoort, located in the center of Holland. Amersfoort was quite picturesque—surrounded by many canals, old castles, and lush forests. In the winter, when the canals were frozen and the ice was strong, we children could go to school on our ice skates, taking shortcuts and having lots of fun at the same time.

I was the youngest of four children, born of Jewish parents in the city of Rotterdam. My oldest brother, Jes (Ies), was nineteen years my senior. Then came my next brother, Ben, ten years older than I, followed by my sister, Elisabeth, who was nine years older. My father's parents, sisters, and brothers also lived in Rotterdam. It was a large family! I remember many Sunday mornings when all of us assembled at my grandparents' home waiting in line to pay our respects to my grandmother. My grandfather had passed away long before.

My mother was very beautiful; she had married my father when she was nineteen. I adored her. She was soft-spoken, gentle, and an attentive listener. I was extremely attached to her. When I was five years old, my father died in an accident. It left my mother devastated. It was then that she decided to move to Amersfoort to be near her parents and siblings.

My mother's parents, my beloved grandparents Oma and Opa, were very religious and helped to raise me in the Jewish Orthodox fashion. When I turned six years old I began Hebrew school and shortly thereafter learned to read Hebrew.

My school, called "De Meisjes School," was an all-girls school located on a plateau, called "Het Plantsoen," near an old castle. My teachers were quite strict; the headmistress, especially, was to be awed and feared. However, all of those who attended De Meisjes School, received an excellent education, including learning the languages of our neighboring countries. In the fourth grade, we started to learn French, followed by English in the fifth grade, and German in the sixth grade. I disliked mathematics but loved languages, which were taught, as was the custom, by teachers from the particular countries where these languages were spoken. I shall always be grateful for this education, which served me well throughout my life.

I attended school each day from nine in the morning until noon, and from two to four in the afternoon, with the exception of Wednesdays and Saturdays. On Wednesdays, we attended school half-day, and I did not go to school on Saturdays, which was the Holy Sabbath. On the Sabbath I went with my grandfather to the Synagogue. This was an exciting event for me because afterwards my sister and I went home to join my mother, grandmother, aunts and uncles for a plentiful luncheon. We sang Hebrew songs of grace and enjoyed sweets, and I savored the feeling of safety and security with my family in this warm and loving atmosphere.

My grandfather was very handsome; he was tall and blond and very dignified-looking. I remember how, on our way to the Synagogue, people greeted him with reverence. One of my favorite memories is my grandfather reading the daily newspaper aloud to my grandmother, whose eyes were not in good condition. The love they shared between them was enviable.

My birthday was celebrated on St. Nicolaas Day, December 5, although my real birthday is December 3. St. Nicolaas Day (in Dutch, Sinterklaas Dag) in Holland is always celebrated with much joy, fun, and surprises. Legend has it that St. Nicolaas arrives on a ship from Spain and, after embarking, mounts a white horse. With his Moorish helpers, he visits schools and homes in the township. No matter what religion one observed, Sinterklaas Dag was celebrated by all.

My sister, Elisabeth, age 15

My brother Ies' wife, Elisabeth (also nicknamed Bep)

So on this particular day, skating home, I was very much looking forward to Sinterklaas Dag, birthday presents, and my school's upcoming chorale presentation. I remember being quite excited! However, as I approached my home, a funny feeling came over me that I couldn't explain. All through my life, I would experience this feeling again and again as a warning of impending doom.

My mother greeted me at the door with tears streaming down her face. She took me in her arms and as she held me, my sister, who stood nearby, said, "Opa died." This was a terrible blow for all of us.

"What do you mean?" I said. "Opa cannot die." But I had lost my beloved grandfather. I remember the funeral, attended by all who knew him: dignitaries, friends, family, neighbors. The mourning period lasted seven days, and during that time people would come in and out of my grandparents' house with food—especially egg dishes because eggs were regarded as the symbol of life.

After my grandfather died, I watched my grandmother gradually deteriorate. Within a half year, she too passed away.

When I was ten years old, my oldest brother, Ies, married a local girl. My mother had hoped that Ies would have waited awhile so he could concentrate on helping her make decisions for the family. My other brother, Ben, had left home to live in Amsterdam with a family who was teaching him a trade. Nevertheless, Ies and his bride had a beautiful wedding.

The wedding was held in the local Synagogue with all of our family and friends in attendance. I vividly remember the beautiful dresses that my sister and I wore. Mine was light purple with many flounces, and my sister's was pink, trimmed with white fluff. The festivities continued in my new sister-in-law's home, where my aunt and uncle from Rotterdam presented a fantastic stage play in which they were true professionals. What impressed me most about this event was the singing of the family's history, all in rhyme and to the tune of *The Trop of the Torah*! After each couplet, all of us chanted, "Amen!" My brother Ies also played the piano and the flute quite well. With a family so musically inclined, the festivities lasted until late into the evening. To this day, I have never forgotten this celebration and the intensity and effect it had on me.

After I completed the first six grades of school, I was ready to go on to a higher level of schooling. In Holland, there are several levels of secondary education, depending on the student's abilities and how well he or she performs in the first six grades. I qualified for the Hogere Burger School (HBS), which stands for Higher Education.

After the death of my grandparents in Amersfoort, my mother became increasingly nervous. We ended up selling our house and moving to Amsterdam where my brother, Ben, was living.

My sister, Elisabeth, my mother and me

Chapter 2: Amsterdam

It was a tremendous change for our family, moving from a small town to a big city. I was enrolled in the Joseph Israels H.B.S., a school named for the famous painter who lived from 1824 to 1911.

I soon adjusted to these changes and came to enjoy school. I realize now what a tremendous education I received. Music had always been very important in our family, and the schools of higher learning had a fantastic program that included free musical concerts once or twice each month.

Before these concerts, the principal violinist would visit our class to explain the repertoire. He would discuss the composers, the interpretation of the music, the instruments, the dynamics. When my class attended the concerts at Het Concert Gebouw (the concert hall in the south of Amsterdam), I would listen attentively, understanding and recognizing all I had learned from the principal violinist.

I was most interested in languages. There was a broad spectrum to learn from, including literature and poetry from different countries. Most of all, I enjoyed the literature from South Africa. The Afrikaan language is a variety of Dutch dialects, and the sound is very sweet. The Dutch farmers (the Boers) settled in South Africa around 1836 in the "Great Trek." They helped settle the Orange Free State and the Transvaal. Britain won these territories in the Boer War of 1899–1902. When our class learned about South Africa, we always began our lessons with a song, and we often sang with great gusto the folksong "Sari Marijs."

During these school years I spent my summer vacations with my oldest brother and his wife in Amersfoort. My ties with my hometown were still very strong. My brother and his wife were a devoted couple, but childless.

My brother Ies

They lived in a modest home, which was a haven of warmth and coziness. They always catered to me and made my stay with them a happy time. They outdid themselves to entertain me with a variety of different events.

Among our favorite outings were bicycle rides through the surrounding villages. One day my sister-in-law said to me, "Let's plan a big trip with the girls (her nieces). Let's go to Doorn and have a picnic. I'll pack up food and drinks."

Doorn, located west of Amersfoort, was a small town, at that time known for its beautiful landscapes. We prepared for the trip and left for Doorn early in the morning, already enjoying our day. We reached Doorn around noon and settled down in the forest for a picnic. As we were laughing and singing, a tall, older gentleman suddenly walked by. We recognized him immediately as the former German Kaiser Wilhelm, who had fled Germany after losing World War I and was exiled to Holland. I distinctly remember how courteously he greeted us as he went on his way. For a few moments we were silent, in awe, but soon continued our singing and fun.

As I later learned, he first lived in the small village of Amerongen, but at the encouragement of our then-Queen Wilhelmina, he settled in an old castle in Doorn. The Dutch, being down-to-earth people, never made a fuss out of Kaiser Wilhelm's living there. Holland had been neutral during the First World War. For us, though, it was quite an experience to see him during our outing.

And so, between school, sports, music, and the fun of growing up, my three years in Amsterdam went by very quickly. I grew up under the reign of Queen Wilhelmina Van Nassau, who was popular among the seven million Dutch people during that time. But there is nothing more permanent than change. Just as I approached my fifteenth birthday, my family was notified that my paternal grandmother had passed away in Rotterdam. My whole family attended her funeral. She had reached a ripe old age, but it was sad for me because now, with the death of this grandmother, I had lost all of the grandparents I loved so much.

After my grandmother's death, and the proper mourning period that followed, we stayed with our family in Rotterdam for a while. We had a large family with many aunts, uncles, and cousins, with whom we all became reacquainted. One day, the oldest brother of my father, my Uncle Saam, asked to speak with us. He was an impressive, stern-looking man who did not mince many words. We might have called him a "no-nonsense man." Although he did not speak much, I distinctly remember that he started or ended each sentence with, roughly translated from the Dutch, "you see," or "don't you see."

In spite of his stern countenance, there was a kindness in his eyes. His opinion was worthy of our trust. He first looked at my mother and said, "You see, now that you are more acquainted with all of the family, I'd like to see you permanently come back to live in Rotterdam." I remember my mother, shy as she was, looking a bit confused and sorrowful. He continued, looking at me now. "You see, your father would have wanted me to be your guardian, and I think it would be best to enroll you in a school where you will continue with languages and learn more practical skills, don't you see. I will be responsible for the two of you and give you advice on everything, you see." My mother nodded shyly, and my uncle ended the conversation with, "I don't like to see you move so much; you need more stability, don't you see?"

I had a tendency to evaluate situations quickly, and my brain began to work overtime. My thoughts went like this: Now I will have a father; I will live here with all of the wonderful family who had spoiled me so much; I will go to a new school. And so my mother and I moved back to Rotterdam that year. My sister lived in the country with a family for whom she worked. My brothers continued to live in Amersfoort and Amsterdam.

Chapter 3: Rotterdam

My mother rented a modest apartment in the center of Rotterdam and enrolled me in a school that specialized in languages and practical arts. This was a good time for my mother and me. Our family was supportive and loving, and my uncle kept his word to us and was generous with good advice. Although my father's side of the family was not religious, my mother could not forget her religious ties with her parents. So my mother and I frequently went to the Synagogue and never missed services on the High Holy Days.

Not far from our new home in Rotterdam, my mother had a half-sister who was married to a famous chessmaster. They and their three sons, like us, loved music. I had taken piano lessons since I was seven years old and could play quite well. With great enthusiasm, my three cousins, some friends, and I formed a musical group. It was great fun, and our families encouraged us and enjoyed listening to our performances.

About this time I began to bloom, and when I was fifteen my mother enrolled me in a Jewish youth club, the JJK. This club offered many activities, including tennis, sailing, swimming, and ballet. In addition, through this club I attended lectures and book reviews by renowned speakers. I remember with great nostalgia when a group of us went sailing on the Kralingsche Plas, which was a lake in the northeast section of Rotterdam. One of the group members brought records, and all of us teenagers became mesmerized by the soothing melodies of the American jazz singers. We all sang along to the tune "Up a Lazy River" and other melodies from the musical *Forty Second Street,* as well as other great American musicals.

I made a lot of friends, and with the approval of our parents we often went by car to the Kurhaus, a fine music hall in the resort town of

Scheveningen, on the North Sea. Our excursions were always cultural, and my mother, being a wonderful person, was happy for me when she knew I was having a good time. I adored her.

But nothing lasts forever, it seems. By that time many Jewish families from Germany had settled in Holland. My mother began to talk about Hitler and how his burgeoning power would affect the Jewish population. But she always ended these discussions with "But nothing will happen in Holland because the queen is here. And Holland always stays neutral."

Chapter 4: The Foreboding Years

The Netherlands is so-called because it is located below sea level on the North Sea. With Germany to the east, Denmark to the north, Belgium, Luxembourg, and France to the south, my family became quite familiar with the different languages of our neighbors.

My ancestors had lived in Holland since the beginning of the seventeenth century, and Jews had lived in Holland long before that time. In 1806, Holland was occupied by King Louis, brother of Napoleon. The Jewish people under his reign enjoyed freedom of religion; however, they were required to take surnames. Historically, Jews had been given first names. They were known only as, for example, so-and-so, son of, or daughter of. During this time in Holland, they were required to take on a last name. Most Jews chose the name of their profession or the name of a street or a canal.

King Louis, or Lodewijk in Dutch, became so popular that his brother Napoleon became jealous and thought Louis too independent. In 1810, Napoleon decided to annex Holland. After four years as King of Holland, Louis fled to Austria. In 1815, William of Orange became King William the First of Holland, a country now free from France.

There are still many French words and expressions in the Dutch language. For example, the Dutch motto Je Maintiendrai is in French and means "I shall maintain." This motto appears on all military and police uniforms and dates back to when King Louis Napoleon was King of Holland from 1806 to 1810.

In the fifteenth and sixteenth centuries, thousands of Spanish and Portuguese Jews fled to Holland to escape the Spanish Inquisition. They

My cousin, Colonel J. deLange (retired); notice the Je Maintiendrai logo on his uniform

were lovingly welcomed by the Dutch. These Sephardic (Spanish) Jews brought much trade to Holland. The shrewd Dutch people recognized and welcomed this. In later years, some streets in Holland were named after these Jews who contributed so much to the economy of my country.

The Portuguese built a beautiful Synagogue in Amsterdam, which is still in use. They also produced great philosophers, writers, painters, and scientists, all of whom added much culture to Holland.

As Jews, we felt more than secure living in Holland under the reign of Queen Wilhelmina. I cannot recall any hint of anti-Semitism during the time of my youth, although Hitler was gaining in power.

My brother Ben was blessed with having great vision and a keen knowledge of politics. I remember how he had lectured my mother on the case of Vander Lubbe, a Dutch wanderer who was falsely accused by the Germans of having set the Reichstag (Parliament building) in Berlin on fire. The then-president of Germany, Von Hindenburg, was becoming quite old and elected Adolph Hitler as chancellor of Germany. Vander Lubbe was killed by the Germans, and with the burning of the Reichstag and the majority of Germans voting for Hitler's party, Hitler began to make laws to his own liking. In 1933, he proclaimed himself the Führer of Germany.

One day in 1935, my mother said, "We have to take in and help a German family." I did not quite understand the situation at that time. Then my mother added, "Hitler is not friendly to the Jews, but we won't have to worry because Holland will remain neutral. Besides, the queen will protect us." But clouds were appearing on the horizon with Hitler gaining more and more power.

And so we took a Jewish couple into our home. As we listened to their plight and to the frightening accounts of what was going on in Germany, we found it very difficult to perceive of such destruction of Jewish lives and property. In school I had learned what a cultured and refined country Germany was—home to so many intellectuals. Now, the seemingly impossible was happening. Here I was, in my blossoming adolescence, already questioning whether one can always believe what one is taught.

Felix

Chapter 5: A Meeting of Importance

I was not too fond of the German couple who was staying with us. They seemed to upset the serenity of our home. The husband was demanding and forceful, I was used to my mother's gentleness. However, my sports activities and schooling compensated for the tension at home. I was fond of tennis and spent most Sunday mornings on the tennis courts.

One day, a handsome young man approached me and asked if I would play a doubles set with him and two of his friends. Flattered, I immediately said yes! I was impressed with this tall, interesting man with the strange accent who paid a lot of attention to me. He introduced himself; his name was Felix. After the tennis match we went to the clubhouse to enjoy a friendly chat. I learned that Felix was from Germany and with one of his brothers had come to Holland several years before. The next week I met Felix again for more games of tennis. Afterward he invited me for a walk.

The year was now 1937; I remember it was a beautiful summer day. We walked for a long time engaged in animated conversation. At one point, we stopped at a teahouse for some lemonade. Here he discussed politics with me. I must admit, I was not too interested and found that I was somewhat unfamiliar with what was happening in other countries. This was difficult for Felix to understand.

After many Sundays of playing tennis, I invited Felix to our home. My mother and brother were as impressed with him as I was. Felix had a deep understanding of history, and I found I was learning a lot from him. He told me his mother still lived in Germany at this time, but his sister was already living in Holland.

I became very pensive in the months following my meeting Felix. He introduced me to his friends who also had fled Germany. Each one had a horror story to tell. As the year sped by, the tension in Germany became worse and worse. In March 1938, German troops marched into Austria. After assassinating Chancellor Dollfuss, Hitler annexed Austria with Germany. All of the bad news at that time seemed to have come to a climax. In 1938, Hitler invaded Sudetenland, a part of Czechoslovakia. Felix and his brother and sister were adamant about getting their mother out of Germany. They said it was time for her to leave.

As time went on, I became quite attached to Felix. My family and I were in awe of his knowledge concerning world events. I began to develop a certain feeling of security whenever we were together. I told myself that I was not afraid. I tried to suppress my fear and nervousness, which seemed to grow with each new horror story that I heard about Hitler and his treatment of Jews. One day as Felix and I were walking, I said to him, "As long as the queen is here, I am not afraid." He gave me a sorrowful look, and with a frown on his face, he replied, "Let me tell you something. Don't think for a moment that Hitler is afraid of your queen. Believe me when I say that things don't look good for the Jews in Europe." Remembering the words of my mother, I said, "Holland will remain neutral. How can things ever change here?" Felix turned to me with a sad smile. "You are too naive to understand the situation." He then kissed me softly on the lips. With that, we went on our way.

Our lives went on, but I became rather introverted. I kept thinking, "How is it possible, these things that are happening? It is almost 1938 and we are not living in the Middle Ages any longer. Why should things like this happen in a civilized world? Germany is a refined country. The German people will not allow Hitler to go on this way."

Now it was time to get Felix's mother out of Germany. He told me about the picturesque village he was from in the south of Germany, located in a beautiful valley, surrounded by mountains and rivers. His family had lived there for many generations raising their children in the peaceful setting. Meanwhile, Hitler had declared all Jews stateless. Felix needed a new

Felix's mother

passport to enter Germany and had to go to the German Consulate in Amsterdam to apply for one. They declared him stateless and gave him the passport with a big *J* (Jew) stamped on it!

When he arrived at his village in Germany, he found his mother bewildered by the circumstances. She wanted to stay in her home. Felix explained what was happening in Germany and finally convinced her to go with him and leave everything behind. She left with tears streaming down her face, forced to say good-bye to the village and the home that she loved so much.

The lives of the Jewish people in Holland had also become frantic and chaotic. Many Jews wanted to leave Holland, but where would they go? It

The picturesque village, Sennfeld (Baden), in Germany where Felix was born

was difficult to immigrate to America. One needed visas to go to another European country. Some people had the opportunity to go to England. Others thought of Switzerland where they had funds in bank deposits.

By now it was the fall of 1938. During this time, thousands of Jewish people from both Germany and Austria were arrested and sent to concentration camps. A young man named Grunspan, the son of Polish Jews, had killed the secretary of the German Embassy in Paris, Ernest Von Rath, because Grunspan's parents had been deported. In revenge, many Germans began what was called *Kristallnacht,* or "the breaking of the glass night." *Kristallnacht* was fueled, of course, by Hitler. Synagogues as well as businesses and homes owned by Jews were destroyed, and thousands of Jewish people from both Germany and Austria were arrested and sent to concentration camps. My mother, my sister and I were agonized with fear.

One evening, Felix came to our home and said, "I am not staying in Holland." He and his brother had prominent positions with a family-owned import/export grain company that had a branch in Rotterdam, and the company would help him to leave Holland. I clearly remember asking him, "What about England and France? Why don't they stop Hitler?" "These countries are not prepared for war yet," he replied. "Mr. Chamberlain is in contact with Hitler." When these conversations took place in my home, I tried to change my foreboding thoughts and forced myself to think of pleasant things. But the horror of it all would not go away—not in our part of the world and not in my mind.

One evening in May of 1939, Felix came to visit my family. The expression on his face as he entered our home was foreboding: something important was about to take place.

Me with my mother before leaving Holland

Chapter 6: Leaving Holland

Felix had received word from family who still lived in Germany that they had finally found a way to get out. They had obtained visas to go to Cuba, a country that had given German refugees permission to enter. Of course, large sums of money were exchanged for these permits at the Cuban Embassy, but at that time, people would give up anything to get out of Germany and save their lives. On the evening of May 13, 1939, the biggest ship of the German company HAPAC, the SS *St. Louis*, left Hamburg with about one thousand people on board. The *St. Louis* was destined for Cuba.

Among the people aboard were writers, scientists, doctors, professors, and other intellectuals. Felix's family eagerly anticipated leaving a country that would destroy Synagogues, burn books, destroy Jewish homes, and throw innocent people in concentration camps. It was clearly a country gone insane. But their anticipation was tinged with much sorrow. Some people had to leave their parents or older members of their families behind. They had to say farewell to their homes, their possessions, and a country where they had lived their whole life.

As the *St. Louis* approached the harbor in Havana, word came to the ship that the authorities would not let it dock. People began to panic; some wanted to jump overboard. The tension became unbearable. Finally, the Cuban authorities ordered the ship to return to Germany within twenty-four hours. Panic, chaos, and dread ensued.

As the ship made its way back, the coast of Florida came into view. Passengers could already see the skyscrapers of Miami in the distance. In a state of desperation, the captain of the SS *St. Louis* communicated by telegram with authorities in the United States.

When the ship reached the coast of Florida, the passengers were full of hope and excitement, convinced that the United States would allow them to embark. But after days of negotiating, America refused to take the refugees in. There was no help for the *St. Louis*. The ship sailed back to Germany—a destination of death for all aboard.

Holland took in about two hundred of these people, among them, one of Felix's relatives. Belgium and France also took in some passengers, but the remainder of the passengers were sent back to Germany where they later perished in the concentration camps. It was now June of 1939, and what should have been a serene summer began to take on apocalyptic dimensions.

Felix, whose company was located in Rotterdam, had indicated that it would do anything to get him out of Holland. Our relationship was pure friendship, and I felt a deep respect for him. My entire family was touched by his sincerity. The German couple whom we had helped had left for Belgium. We never heard from them again. In the meantime, we met people from Austria, Czechoslovakia, and Germany. Those who managed to escape told us horrifying stories. Those who opposed Hitler's policies were rounded up and sent to concentration camps in various parts of Germany.

The summer came and went. I stopped reading the newspapers. I only looked at the headlines each day to know what was happening. The entire time I carried a flicker of hope that things would change. They did not. On September 1, 1939, Hitler invaded the western part of Poland after he had made a secret agreement with the USSR that it would occupy the eastern part of Poland.

Now that Hitler, the self-proclaimed Führer, had broken his promise for peace and resorted to continued aggression, England and France declared war on Germany during the first week of September 1939. It was dreadful—neighboring countries at war with each other? Germany, the refined country I had admired through my studies at school, was the malicious aggressor? How naive of me! Hadn't I learned all about World War I in school? To hide my fear, I still clung to the idea that Holland would stay out of the war; that we would, as my mother always said, "stay neutral."

Then one evening in late October of 1939, Felix visited our home. He was serious and somber and asked to speak with my mother alone. My sister and I insisted on staying in the room with them. "I have come to tell you that I just received a telegram from my company's office in Buenos Aires," he began. "They have arranged a visa for me for South America." He continued, facing my mother, "You know by now that I am a serious, down-to-earth person. I have read *Mein Kampf* and I can judge what the Nazi movement is all about. I will leave Holland in a few weeks. I'm booking on a Dutch neutral ship. The idea is to go to Chile and from there to Argentina where the headquarters of my company are located. The name of the ship that will take me there is the SS *Simon Bolivar*."

We listened intently and tried to take it all in, but it was difficult to comprehend all that was about to happen with our beloved friend Felix. My mother was about to speak, but Felix interrupted. "I want to point out that there is much danger ahead of us. I feel that it is totally possible for the Germans to invade Holland." I had not taken it seriously when in the past Felix told me he would leave Holland. But that evening I was shocked. He was really leaving! My family would lose our "rock," which is what Felix had become.

I looked at my mother's face, so dear to me. Her beautiful face was full of sorrow. It is amazing that at times like these, especially during moments of silence, one observes so many small details. For instance, I remember that night it was raining very hard. The clatter against the window, the gush of the wind, the quiet pounce of the cat jumping onto my mother's lap, the internal sound of my heart pounding—I was acutely aware of these sounds that invaded our silence. That horrible foreboding feeling, the same feeling I had the day Opa died, overwhelmed me once again. It seemed so long ago.

Felix took my hand in his, which caused me to leave my sad pondering and pay full attention to what was happening. His next words stunned me—and left everyone in my family speechless. "I can take Flory with me, even if we are not married. I can save her life and I promise you that I will take care of her. At least she will not fall into the hands of the Nazis."

No one spoke. No one could. What Felix was proposing would alter the course of my life. Finally, my sister broke the silence. "We will have to talk

Photo taken just before Felix and I left Holland

to the family first," she said. Felix turned to face my mother and spoke directly to her. "I know it is a big responsibility on my part, but this is better than falling prey to the Nazis." My mother nodded. "But first," he continued, "I must know if Flory wants to come with me. She is the one we are talking about. I give you my word, I will take good care of her."

The silence became so unbearable that just to break it I coughed a bit. I felt so sorry for my mother; her face looked pale and haunted. Once again my sister said, "We have to discuss it with the family." Felix turned to her and said, "Let's first make sure that Flory wants to come with me. Then I will talk to your family and explain what my plans are." With a stern face he continued, "But I must have an answer soon. The time element is urgent and the ship will sail in a few weeks."

I felt numb. It took a long while before I had absorbed the idea of leaving Holland, leaving my darling mother, my beloved family, and the country that I loved so much. I became totally confused—torn about staying on. Felix embraced me. Suddenly I blurted out, "I want to go with Felix." He repeated once again, "I will take good care of her." After Felix left, I could feel the emotions of the evening coming to a climax. I knew I had to stick with my decision.

The next day we had another meeting at our house. My brothers, my sister, and my uncle, who was also my guardian, were all there. After Felix discussed his plans, my oldest brother, Ies, said to no one in particular, "I hope you know what you are doing." My brother Ben, the one with vision, turned to Felix and said, "It is a good idea to leave if you can make it. Remember, there is a war going on." My uncle made an attempt to speak and started to say, "Don't you see," but by then everyone had begun to talk at once. Ben said, "If America comes in, the war might be over soon. Hitler must be stopped. Felix knows what he is doing."

"Yes," I said. "I want to go with Felix."

We all kissed each other, cried, and hugged. The atmosphere was a mix of emotions: sadness, excitement, hope for the future. And so when Felix and the others had left, I went to my room to face a sleepless night. But the next morning I focused my thoughts on the future, and I put my trust in Felix.

SS Simon Bolivar

THE ODYSSEY OF THE
SS *SIMON BOLIVAR*

Chapter 7: Tragedy at Sea

Within a few days Felix had booked two cabins on the SS *Simon Bolivar,* an 8,300-ton passenger ship of the Royal Dutch Shipping Company, or Koninklyke Nederlandsche Stoomboot Maatschappy. Destined for Curacao (Netherlands Antilles), the ship would sail on Friday night, November 17, 1939, from Ijmuiden. From there it would go to Chile.

With the onset of winter the trees were losing their leaves. It rained constantly. The days seemed shorter, and the darkness set in as early as the afternoon. There was much to do! I admit that sometimes I was enthusiastic and other times quite sad. The whole situation became so confusing. I hated the Germans for upsetting the world. I needed to decide what to pack and what to leave. My feelings tugged at me. I wanted to get away from the war, and yet I did not want to leave my mother and family.

German planes had already been spotted over Holland. The news around the world was grim; the tension became unbearable at times. Finally, the time had come for me to leave. We were to travel to Amsterdam and from there to Ijmuiden, where the ship would set sail.

At my home we had said our tearful good-byes to our families—to my mother, sister and brothers, and Felix's family. At the railway station in Rotterdam, many friends and other relatives came to see us off. Some of my family members whom I loved most were not there because it was the Holy Sabbath, the day of the week when they would not travel. It was Friday night, Shabbat.

A prayer for our well-being was recited, and my mother and Felix's mother gave us their blessings. After all this, the emotions became too difficult for us to bear, and we finally boarded the train. I could not look back anymore at my mother's dear, sweet face. The train slowly pulled away from the station and we were on our way.

On the way to Amsterdam, we did not speak much because both Felix and I were in a daze. We held hands. Felix did say again to me, "I will take good care of you. All will be well, you'll see."

After we got off the train in Amsterdam, we continued to Ijmuiden, where the SS *Simon Bolivar* was situated in all her glory. Departure was that same night. I was glad; I wanted the time to go by quickly.

We inspected our cabins, checked our luggage, and walked around the ship a bit. I saw on the passenger list that I was to share my cabin with an English girl. There were four hundred people on board, inclusive of the crew. We were served dinner that night, but few could eat under the circumstances. After dinner we went to our cabins to try to take a break from all of the vicissitudes. My roommate was a charming girl who was on her way to Paramaribo, where she worked for an oil company as a secretary. Since I was fluent in English, we chatted amicably until late in the night. I woke up the next morning to a gloomy day. It was Saturday, November 18, 1939. I looked through the porthole of my cabin and noticed dense fog and ominous waters. My roommate was still sleeping soundly.

I was hungry, so I showered, dressed warmly, and left the cabin for breakfast. I met Felix near the staircase on deck. We noticed a lot of children on board, and people were chatting away in different languages: English, Dutch, German. We met other passengers who were also relieved to be able to leave Europe. The morning went by quickly, and after a while, a band began to play music to entertain the passengers. As I listened to the music, I became restless and told Felix that I wanted to go on deck.

Standing on the deck we looked out over the North Sea and sadly thought of our loved ones we had left behind. Soon more people joined us and we became engaged in pleasant conversations—a distraction from our sad thoughts. We learned that there was a fabulous art collection on board, which had been exhibited in the Stedelijk Museum in Amsterdam the previous weeks.

As the weather became colder, I said to Felix, "I'm going to the cabin to get a scarf." On my way, I noticed that a clock on the staircase read 11:20 A.M. I chose a warm shawl out of my suitcase. On my way back to the deck, I gazed at the beautiful wall painting near the staircase. It depicted Simon Bolivar, the courageous liberator of many South American states, after whom the ship was named. He was the person who had kept communications going between Holland and the West Indies.

When I returned to the deck, Felix and a few of the other passengers were involved in a lively conversation about politics. By that time it must have been about 11:45 A.M. Looking out over the water, I noticed something that looked like a tube or a pipe sticking out of the water. I turned to Felix and asked, "How does the captain know the way through all that—"

Before I could finish my sentence there was an enormous explosion. Felix was thrown against the floor of the deck with such force that he could not get up. I also hit the deck floor with such velocity that I could not move. Children were screaming, water was gushing all over, and people were yelling and moaning. Someone from the crew yelled, "Up, up, we have to get up!" Shattered glass was all over the place. It was an apocalypse, a "Dante's Hell."

I turned to see that the young man who had been standing next to me was dead. The grand piano had fallen onto him and several other people. Felix and I could see each other in the midst of the bodies and the turmoil, but we could not communicate. There was blood all over.

Eventually—although I cannot remember how—I managed to crawl over to Felix. Somehow I half-carried him, half-dragged him up the stairs to the highest point of the ship. There, people were screaming, "The captain is dead!" "Where are the life boats?" "Where are my children?" "Where is my wife?" "Send out an S.O.S." We had never rehearsed safety procedures. During the explosion a large piece of glass had hit me in the neck. Blood was everywhere, and it became difficult to hold Felix up; he could not manage to stand on his own.

Within fifteen minutes there was another, even more violent explosion. This time something hit the boiler room of the ship because oil was spouting everywhere. All of us had oil on our hair, faces, and bodies. I saw people running everywhere—people in their pajamas, people half-dressed. There was even a woman naked running for her life. Some were clinging to their little babies; some jumped into the water. By now, the ship was sinking fast. People panicked; there was screaming and chaos everywhere.

When we hit the water, the waves hit us with extreme force. Swimming was out of the question because of the thick layer of oil. Felix and I managed to hang on to a heavy rope. I remember going under water.

In retrospect, I believe it was shear force of will, the rush of adrenaline, and the power of the spirit to stay alive that helped us to hang on to the rope that tragic day. With all of the bones broken in our bodies, it should have been impossible for us to cling so tightly.

What I witnessed that day was a nightmare: people in lifeboats sinking, men and women drowning, babies disappearing into murky waters, people frantically trying to swim.

Shortly after the second explosion, a crew member threw big pieces of wood into the water and several other crew members tried to get some of the lifeboats lowered. It was futile because the second explosion caused many of the lifeboats to disappear along with the people in them.

We clung to the wood and the rope, and I remember going under water several times because I was wearing a heavy coat. Felix kept yelling to me to hang on and not to let go. I was in total shock, not believing it was real. Finally, we were drawn into a lifeboat that was half-filled with water. It was difficult for us to think or collect our thoughts. A man began to pray very loudly. Another man was laying against my legs, blood spurting from his head. He was either dead or unconscious.

Our ship, the majestic SS *Simon Bolivar*, had sunk in a matter of minutes after the second explosion. I looked back from the lifeboat, but there was nothing to see of the ship except for the masts. All I saw were drowning people; there was nothing but death and destruction in a thick shroud of black machine oil.

At that moment, I believed that our ship had been torpedoed. Later we learned that two German mines had caused this terrifying tragedy. Those magnetic mines had been placed there the night before by the German U-boats, *Bernd von Arnim*, *Wilhelm Heidkamp*, and *Hermann Kuenne*. The tragedy on the SS *Simon Bolivar* had claimed the greatest number of lives on any neutral Dutch ship during this period until May 10, 1940.

Our "lifeboat" was quickly filling with water. The sea was so wild that the waters caused it to jerk back and forth, up and down; several times the boat was in a vertical position with all of us hanging on. The wounded man against my legs had rolled over; I was sure he was dead.

I saw that Felix was lying between two other people in the lifeboat. His face was unrecognizable and distorted from pain. I thought to myself, "This is the end. I hope the drowning goes fast."

The nightmare, though, continued. Everyone was praying as loudly as they could. A tall man in the boat said, midway through his prayers, "The captain is dead. He was killed immediately." We were quickly losing hope; there seemed to be no way out of this ordeal.

Darkness began to set in. The fog became even more dense. It seemed as if hours and hours had gone by. What if no one rescued us? I prayed, "Please, God, let it be fast. Let it be over quickly." Suddenly, someone yelled, "A ship, I see a ship!" No one reacted at first, thinking it had been a *fata morgana* (mirage). But there was a ship in the distance! We could see its outline in the midst of the fog. The ship came closer and closer as the tall man in our boat screamed, "It's a British destroyer! We will be saved!" Indeed, it was a British ship. Those on board had heard on their radio that the SS *Simon Bolivar* had been destroyed during an explosion. The ship had spotted us!

Finally after much maneuvering, the destroyer was able to come close to our raft. The British sailors had the impossible task of getting us on board their ship. Of course, they could not approach us too closely for fear they would smash our small raft to pieces. First they threw out lines, but the high waves and the dense fog obstructed their rescue attempts. The crew yelled something to us, but their voices were devoured by the roar of the sea. It was November, very cold, and the rescue seemed like an impossible task. We were beyond help, I thought, hanging on in our wet clothes, drenched in oil, and physically wounded. But praise be to the courageous British sailors—they did not give up on their lifesaving mission.

They persisted, and eventually they lowered cranes into the sea. One by one, the victims were placed in a net. First me and then the men. After our rescue, I did not see Felix again. I later learned that the British sailors, after rescuing Felix and safely positioning him on deck, transported him to the Royal Naval Hospital in Ipswich.

After I was hoisted up, I was placed in a small cabin. A nun, who apparently had also been on the SS *Simon Bolivar*, removed my clothes and dressed me in something belonging to the crew. I remember lying in a bunk and a crew member giving me something warm to drink.

The next few hours were a blur to me. Eventually, I realized I was on a stretcher. Was the ordeal really over? It sank in: I had been rescued. But where was Felix? Was he all right? I also began to think of how the family members of the passengers of the SS *Simon Bolivar* would react once they heard the news of the ship's demise. Later, I learned that we were among the most seriously wounded survivors. Even more devastating, I learned of the strong possibility that someone, knowing many Jews were fleeing Europe, had betrayed the ship's departure time and destination to the Germans, who, I believe, plotted the destruction of the ship. Later I learned that, indeed, a suspicious person had been on board.

This was the fate of those aboard the SS *Simon Bolivar,* the first neutral ship to be sunk in the North Sea, near the English Channel: 104 people had lost their lives. Their hopes and dreams disappeared forever in the depths of the North Sea. I will be forever grateful to the courageous British sailors who gallantly risked their own lives to save ours. Throughout the years we have tried to learn what happened to their ship, which was called

"Greyhound." As we found out later, during times of war, destroyers have no names. We discovered that the Greyhound itself had later been destroyed in the war. The vivid memories of the sailors' bravery will stay with us for as long as we live.

As I lay in the stretcher worrying about Felix, an air raid warning began to sound. People ran away in every direction, but one sailor remained by my side. At that moment, I did not care if I was dead or alive. I heard airplanes flying overhead, and I asked the sailor where I was. He replied, "You are in Harwich; you are safe now. I'll stay here with you." I have never forgotten this. I said to him, "Could you please send a telegram to my family?" He said he would. Frustrated and confused, I could not remember my mother's name or the names of my other family members, or the friends who had accompanied us to the train station upon our departure.

I told the sailor that I could not remember anything. He calmed me down and after the sound of the sirens abated, the name NIDERA, the company where Felix had worked, popped into my head. I requested the sailor to send the telegram to NIDERA in Rotterdam.

Later I found out that, indeed, our families had received the wire informing them that we both had been saved from the demise of the SS *Simon Bolivar.*

By then a terrible excruciating pain had set in my neck and my entire body, and I remembered how I had been hit with a sharp object in my neck and forehead during the first explosion.

Chapter 8: The Dutch Patients

I know at the time I was dazed because after what seemed an interminably long time, I found myself in a hospital bed. Several people hovered over me. They were very friendly and attentive and explained that I was in a small naval hospital in Harwich. They promised that they would take good care of me.

After these people (the doctors and nurses) wrote down many notes regarding my injuries, they wheeled me into an examination room to diagnose my wounds. I must say that the British have a great capacity for remaining calm and putting people at ease. Their kindness was overwhelming as they proceeded. It calmed me down somewhat, although I suffered great anxiety over Felix's fate.

After removing glass from my forehead, they examined my neck again. They called another doctor into the examining room, and they all began to work on my neck. Suddenly, I heard a thud. An object was thrown into a container near where I lay. It was a large piece of glass from the ship's porthole that had become lodged in my neck after the explosion. It was probably the only thing that was left of the SS *Simon Bolivar.* I still have this piece of glass, and keep it in my purse. The two doctors and the nurses were in awe—it was a miracle. The large piece of glass had been lodged just a millimeter away from my carotid artery. I could have died!

The next day my wrist and hand were operated on. The doctors put me in a cast from my hand to my elbow, which I wore for a long time because the fractures were improperly set. Two days later, the nurses attended to my hair, which was a bunch of clustered strings saturated in oil. I had very long hair at that time, and for a long time the nurses were discussing what to do with it. They must have tried a number of chemicals on my hair because when they were done, I was blonde with short hair. I did not recognize myself.

Several days went by, and during the quiet moments I pondered what my fate would be. I had hoped that the friendly sailor who had stayed by my side on the ship had sent the telegram to Rotterdam and that my family knew we had been saved.

I believe it was the third day after I was brought to the hospital that the Dutch ambassador came to visit me at my bedside. He was accompanied by a friendly gentleman by the name of Mr. Bland. They asked me all kinds of questions because, of course, I had no papers, and all we had taken with us on the SS *Simon Bolivar* was now at the bottom of the sea. I told them that I had been on board with my friend Felix, and I relayed as much information as I could. I had hoped that they could bring us together. The English authorities had a tremendous task figuring out who belonged to whom. All the while air raid sirens were going on and off.

Shortly after this, much to my relief and delight, Felix's brother came to the hospital where I was. He had flown over to England from Holland to determine what kind of state we were in. I was so happy to see a familiar face! He promised to find Felix and see to it that we were cared for in the same hospital. It turned out to be a long process because, as I understood much later, we were among the most seriously injured survivors of the ship's explosions. We did not know it then, but we were to remain hospitalized for over six months.

In the meantime, journalists came to see me, filming and interviewing me. I later learned that I had been featured in the news in Holland and that my family had seen me lying in the hospital bed.

But my pain did not subside. Still, I had relentless will power, and I told the doctors that I felt okay, that I must find Felix and go home. During this time I had frequent company. My brother Ben had quite a number of business associates in Liverpool and London, and they all came to the hospital to visit me. Within a few more days, the Dutch ambassador came again and told me that he had located the hospital in Ipswich where Felix

Nieuwe Amsterdamsche Courant

ALGEMEEN HANDELSBLAD

Zondag 19 November 1939

Van de 400 opvarenden:

VIJFTIG ZWAAR EN VIJFTIG LICHT GEWOND NEGENTIG VERMISTEN

310 geredden te Harwich aan land gebracht

Het Ministerie van Buitenlandsche Zaken te 's-Gravenhage heeft gisteravond van Hr. Ms. gezant te Londen telefonisch bericht ontvangen, dat het s.s. „Simon Bolivar" van de Koninklijke Nederlandsche Stoomboot Maatschappij nabij de Engelsche kust op een mijn is geloopen.

Volgens de voorloopige berichten zijn er honderd gewonden te Harwich aan land ge-

HET S.S. „SIMON BOLIVAR".

GESPREKKEN MET GEREDDEN VAN DE „BOLIVAR"

Tweemaal op een mijn? — Nieuwe ontploffing toen de sloepen gestreken werden.

UITERST MOEILIJKE REDDING	GEZAGVOERDER BIJ RAMP GEDOOD
(Van onzen specialen verslaggever.)	Een hofmeester der eerste klasse heeft aan Reuter medegedeeld: „Gezagvoerder Voorewi is ......

The sinking of the SS Simon Bolivar *made news all over the world*

First Assessment of the Royal Navy

"Dutch liner Simon Bolivar *mined 2 miles N.E. of Longsand Head Buoy after being struck by 2 mines at 10 minute intervals. 265 passengers, 140 crew on board, 140 lost approx. The survivors were in a terrible condition from fuel oil, and even the mess decks of the ships in which the survivors were received have been temporarily rendered uninhabitable on account of this. 8 dead, 88 missing, 84 in hospital, 225 survivors,(Adty Deputy Capt. 0758/19) Position about 51° 49-1/2' N. 1° 41' E. Greyhound."*

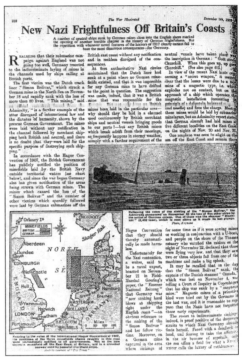

Top left: Transcript of radio transmission
Top right: Article from The War Illustrated
Below: The almost impossible task to save the survivors

was, and soon I would be transferred there. It was so chaotic for the British! They were fighting a war that was steadily becoming worse. The ambassador told me that other ships also either had been torpedoed or sunk because of mines on that same fatal day.

After many days I was transferred to a large hospital in Ipswich, a picturesque British town known as Charles Dickens' residence. There I was to be reunited with Felix. Although I was happy that I would finally be near him, I had become very much attached to the friendly nurses and doctors who cared for me during those two weeks. The farewells and good-byes were tearful for all of us.

Mr. Bland, the gentleman who had accompanied the ambassador during the initial visit, drove me to Ipswich. He promised to take great care of me. At the time, being in pain and under much duress, I simply accepted the generosity of this stranger. It was much later that I realized the true heart and soul of this wonderful man. He was socially prominent and president of Barclay's Bank, one of the largest banks in England. He was deeply concerned about the atrocities caused by Hitler and the war and the pain and suffering of others. Mr. Bland became my guardian angel; I was fortunate to have come under his care. The sinking of the SS *Simon Bolivar*, the first neutral passenger ship to be attacked, made news all over the world.

Finally, finally, I was reunited with my friend Felix. Unfortunately, I found him in terrible shape, although at that moment I did not know the extent of his injuries. A few days later, Mr. Bland introduced me to the head of the hospital, who explained in some detail Felix's condition. I myself had torturous pains all over, but I did not want to succumb to my agony.

I was led to an office where I met Felix's doctor. Mr. Bland advised me to address him as "mister" and not "doctor." In England medical specialists are not referred to as "doctor." "Mister" connotes greater prestige.

I vividly remember the tall, good-looking gentleman who spoke to me and Mr. Bland. First, the doctor reiterated the terrible ordeal Felix and I had been through and expressed his concern. He then told me about Felix's injuries. Felix had broken his pelvis and damaged his urinary tract, which caused terrible pain and made it impossible for him to urinate normally. We had a long conversation, and the doctor even drew some diagrams for me so I would better understand Felix's injuries.

However, I did not understand the seriousness of Felix's condition until the doctor said, frowning, "I must let you know that your friend is so seriously wounded that there is a great possibility he will never walk again." I must have begun to cry because both men patted me on the back, and the doctor said in a consoling tone, "It is best that you do not tell Felix this. I can assure you that we here in Ipswich will do our utmost to get him well." And with that I went back to Felix's ward. I did not reveal to him the devastating news I had just heard.

It was now the end of November and the weather was bitter cold. Felix and I were under the care of a special nurse whose compassion was enormous. She went out of her way to make us comfortable. In time she became like a second mother to me; I grew to love her dearly. I was still in my teens and in need of a lot of reassurance. Her name was Sister Jeannie, and I have never forgotten her.

Of the two of us, Felix suffered the most. He was placed flat on his back in bed with two heavy sandbags on either side of his body to keep him from moving. As for myself, my injuries caused me so much pain and inconvenience that I could not stand it any longer. Mr. Bland, who visited us every day, noticed my agony. One day he took me aside in the hospital lobby and said in a serious tone, "I'm going to take you to the best physician, a bone specialist. I know he can help you."

The next day he made an appointment for me with this specialist, who would give me a complete physical examination. I was ambivalent about the scheduled appointment because by then I had convinced myself that my body would heal on its own.

I had many worries accumulating. Family and friends had written to me that my mother had taken the news of our disaster very badly. I so much wanted to go home, back to Holland, back to my mother. But this would not happen for a long time.

Mr. Bland took me to the bone specialist, Mr. Jones. His staff took lots of x-rays, examined me for a long time, and discovered that I had multiple fractures of my ribs, knee, and wrist that had not been set properly. Because of the heavy explosions I was thrown on the deck of the SS *Simon Bolivar* so furiously that I had suffered multiple fractures on the left side of my body. My knee had also been injured during the explosion at sea. The next day I was put in a body cast! I was not required to remain immobile in bed, but the cast caused me great difficulty in walking. I had to hobble. Because there were so many seriously injured military people in the hospital, the medical staff needed all of the beds available. Besides, I was young and had amazing will power and was determined to get around by myself.

Mr. Jones advised me to undergo another operation on my wrist. But I was so fearful of the crude anesthetic that I adamantly refused. I vividly remember him saying, "You are a silly girl." He was right; I have been sorry all my life that I did not heed his advice. Not only would my wrist look deformed to me later in my life, but playing the piano with that hand was extremely difficult.

But now there was the issue of what to do with me next. My guardian angel, Mr. Bland, told me that Felix would have to remain in the hospital for a long time. "So why don't I see to it," he said, "that you are set up in a boarding home where you can comfortably recuperate." I liked the idea, and within a few days he came to the hospital to tell me that he had found the perfect place. Although I was a little anxious and worried, this move turned out to be a good experience for me.

The boarding house was owned and operated by a Miss Morling, a sweet, kind, elderly woman. I clearly remember Mr. Bland insisting how important it was to take good care of me. I assume that the fact that he was president of Barclay's Bank impressed Miss Morling because I felt as if the red carpet was rolled out for me. The house was a typical English country home surrounded by many large trees and lush bushes. At that time of the year there were no flowers in bloom, but one could imagine, even during the cold winter, how lovely the grounds would look in spring and summer.

Miss Morling's guests were all young people. I had to share my bedroom with another girl whose name was Emma. I remember she was very beautiful with flaming red hair. She was also sweet, kind, and helpful to

Miss Morling

me. She reminded me of my roommate on the SS *Simon Bolivar* with whom I had shared a cabin for only one night, whose hopes and dreams were now at the bottom of the sea. Each time I thought of her, tears came to my eyes.

There was only one open fireplace in the house located in the living room. I had to share the bed with Emma, but we didn't mind because the temperature was so cold at night—it felt as if the thermometer fell way below zero degrees! Emma had to get up very early in the morning to go to work. We each had a jar with water to wash ourselves; we always washed very quickly and then went to the open fireplace to warm ourselves. I hobbled along with Emma, who helped me down the stairs. Mr. Bland came to visit me each morning promptly at 8:30; I could have set my clock by his visits. He was very concerned about my well-being.

Miss Morling had a cheerful manner that was contagious. For some reason she nicknamed me Dolly and called me her "little Dutch Dolly." One morning, many days after I had arrived at her boarding house, she said to me, "How would you like to go for a walk?" I was eager to get out, and I enthusiastically accepted her invitation. She continued, "We can walk to the hospital. You will see that it is not far." And so we went, Miss Morling walking beside me as I hobbled along in my body cast.

When we arrived at the hospital, we went through the long corridors to get to Felix's room. Poor Felix was in constant pain. There was nothing we could do for him; we were all helpless. At that time we did not have the medical research and technology we have today. But we did have Nurse Jeannie who did her best to cheer us up. While we were visiting Felix that day, Nurse Jeannie said to me, "Do you know there are Dutch sailors from the SS *Simon Bolivar* in the next ward?" She led us through another corridor. What a surprise! Four or five Dutch people from the crew of the ship were lying there. We all began to talk at once. They too had suffered multiple fractures, but were not as badly hurt as Felix.

I so much enjoyed talking with them! The Dutch are accustomed to eating a lot, and they asked us if we had access to food stores. Of course we said we would try to get them what they wanted and be back the next day. On the way back to the boarding home, I apologized to Miss Morling for talking for so long in my native language to the sailors. She said she did not mind, so I recounted the entire conversation to her in English.

As young and naive as I was, the next day I decided I could go to the hospital on my own. Miss Morling was very reluctant so I said to her, "Ask Mr. Bland's opinion." The next day she did, but Mr. Bland frowned and told me quite firmly that he felt I should wait a few more days. With all the air raids, I needed to know my way around much better than I did.

Though there were strict visiting hours at the hospital, Nurse Jeannie allowed me to visit any time because she knew how much I wanted to be with Felix. I never divulged a word to him about what his doctor discussed with me, but I continued to worry about his progress. I later discussed the matter with Mr. Bland. He looked pensive and said, "I've spoken with Felix's physician. His injuries are very serious and might take a long time to heal." I felt a slight panic set in until Mr. Bland reassured me. "Be patient," he continued. "I promise that we here in England will take good care of both of you. You'll have the best care possible. Don't worry. It will be all right." With that, he left me in the good care of Miss Morling.

By now it was the end of December; we had been in England for over a month. Christmas and New Year's were approaching. I had become more or less accustomed to my life with darling Miss Morling hovering over me and Mr. Bland supervising. Some of the boarders had gone home for the Christmas season, among them my roommate Emma. I missed her very much. She helped me climb the stairs every night, which was a difficult task for me with my cast. Besides, it was pleasant to talk with her before going to sleep.

From time to time, Mr. Bland took me to his country home. It was a beautiful, large estate located on acres of exquisitely landscaped property—something out of a British movie. The facade of the house took my breath away when I saw it for the first time.

Mrs. Bland was a charming woman. She, her husband, and family welcomed me graciously on my first visit. The inside of their home was as tasteful as the outside. In particular, I remember their library. The walls were adorned with beautifully framed paintings that, Mr. and Mrs. Bland explained to me, had been in the family for centuries. There were paintings of their ancestors as well as masterpieces acquired from famous painters.

Back at the boarding house, Miss Morling was getting ready for Christmas. She took me with her to buy a modest Christmas tree, which I helped her trim and decorate. Walking was still awkward for me, and the cast felt very cold on my body. Despite this, I was swept away in the gaiety of it all and in the atmosphere Miss Morling created. I was thinking that at this time of year it was also Hanukkah, the Festival of Lights and the Festival of Freedom and Dedication. I was sure that no one in Ipswich knew what Hanukkah was. And so, as the saying goes, "When in Rome, do as the Romans do." So I joined in the celebration of Christmas, mostly because I genuinely loved Miss Morling. We felt very comfortable in each other's company in spite of our different religions.

Miss Morling was fond of the hymns in her *Alexander's Prayer Book*. I played them on the organ that stood in the living room, although the cast on my wrist did not allow me to play my very best. On Sundays before the Christmas season began, all of the boarders had dinner together. Miss Morling always served the same dinner: mutton, Yorkshire pudding, and dessert. A wonderful aroma filled the air, and all of us would sit around the open fire singing songs from the hymnal. Despite the occasional air raids, these evenings radiated peace and harmony.

Just before Christmas I received an unexpected surprise—something of a gift! Early one morning the doorbell rang. When Miss Morling opened the door, a gentleman in a naval officer's uniform stood there. He identified himself as a crew member of the destroyer that had rescued survivors of the SS *Simon Bolivar*. He had found out that I was living in the boarding home, and he asked Miss Morling if he could say hello to me. She hesitated at first, but he seemed honest so she let him in and called me.

When I came into the living room, I was thrilled to see the officer who had stood by me on the platform in Harwich when the air raid sirens went off and everyone else went running. What a meeting! We hugged, and I cried and thanked him over and over again. He told me that he had in fact sent the telegram of our rescue to Rotterdam, as I had asked him to do. When I asked him his name, he identified himself only as "James." He explained that he could not divulge the name of the destroyer, or where he came from. After all, a war was going on; secrets had to be kept. But on that morning we rejoiced. I told him all about Felix. Unfortunately, our visit was short. After he left I never saw or heard from him again.

That afternoon I went to the hospital and told Felix about my surprise. He was still in much pain, and I stayed with him a long time, unaware that evening had come and darkness had set in. When I said good-bye to Felix, I quickly went to the Dutch sailors' ward to say hello. When I left the hospital, I saw that fog had set in. As I walked away, an air raid suddenly went off, which meant that I had to stay where I was. I recall that it was quite awhile before I could continue homeward, but now I had lost my way. It was terrifying! Everything was pitch dark. I went first in one direction, then another, up and down different streets, until I realized I was truly lost. Panic set in until I finally ran into someone to whom I explained my predicament. Luckily, he was a constable and immediately escorted me to the boarding house. By this time it was quite late, and Miss Morling had already sent her young men out to find me.

This was such a harrowing experience that even now at the time of this writing, I become uneasy remembering this frightening experience. Both of us, Felix and I, must have had a guardian angel watching over us.

Felix's brother, Theo

Chapter 9: Exit England

Christmas and New Year's came and went. It was now 1940. All of Miss Morling's boarders were back, including Emma, and I was glad to see them again. We often spoke about Hitler and the countries he had occupied, and it was frightening for me to look ahead to the future. I admired my small circle of friends in Ipswich; they never seemed to show any fear. In the meantime, two more boarders were called to military duty.

The first two months of 1940 went by rather uneventfully. Again I visited my doctor, Mr. Jones, who told me that soon my cast would come off. As far as Felix was concerned, they would try to get him out of bed in a few weeks. In the meantime, Theo, Felix's brother, visited us again. He advised us to try to stay in England. Of course, Felix, in the condition he was in, could hardly move, let alone leave England.

Finally at the end of February, my cast came off. It felt very strange at first, and I was dizzy. Mr. Jones still strongly recommended resetting my wrist to correct the problem, but I did not feel like having another operation. He warned me that my wrist would never be the same.

The month of March approached, and one afternoon Nurse Jeannie told me that the hospital staff would try to get Felix out of bed the next morning when Mr. Jones would be there. I remember being quite excited, and I arrived at the hospital very early the next morning. When Mr. Jones came into Felix's room, the anticipation was palpable. I know it was quite a painful ordeal for Felix, but he was able to stand on his own feet for a few moments. And what a moment that was for all of us!

Mr. Jones came to see Felix every day. He ordered a therapist who could help Felix perform exercises to strengthen his body so he could walk again. We all held our breath for many, many days. It was the love and encouragement of all of the nurses and doctors that finally, finally, at the beginning of April 1940, got Felix to slowly walk down the hospital corridors on his own.

Of course we had to be patient, but now, Felix and I could at least contemplate the next steps we would take toward our future. We had been in England for five and one-half months in and out of hospitals. All I could think of was going back to my mother, but Felix thought it wiser to remain in England until we could try again to go to South America.

Around the second week of April, Miss Morling came to my room waving a newspaper. She looked distressed as she said to me in a worried tone, "Dolly, Hitler has invaded Denmark and Norway. France and England are sending troops . . . Oh, my goodness," she lamented, "Where will all this lead to?" Shortly after, all the young men in the boarding house had to report for military duty overseas.

By the end of April Felix could walk well enough so that he was able to do a few things for himself. Mr. Bland suggested that Felix stay at Miss Morling's boarding home so he could fully recuperate. I remember the day Felix arrived at Miss Morling's. In spite of his physical limitations at the time, Felix resorted to his old active self. He wasted no time trying to get in touch with the authorities to get a permit to stay in England. But this was not to be. Felix was a native of Germany, and that was enough reason for the British to refuse him a permanent stay. Even though Felix was at the boarding home, he was still under the doctor's care every day. I was glad that I had never told Felix about the doctor's original prognosis that he might not walk again. Our guardian angel again helped him to defy this fate.

Now the time had come for Felix and me to start talking about arrangements to return to Holland. In the shipwreck we had lost all of our possessions, and we had no insurance. The shipping company, Koninklyke Nederlandsche Stoomboot Maatschappy—the Royal Dutch Shipping Company—had, of course, paid for our stay and our medical care in England. Now they had to plan our return. We now knew that Denmark and Norway had been invaded by Hitler at the beginning of April. Traveling by ship was too dangerous; thus, arrangements were made for us to return to Holland by airplane.

One morning, Miss Morling came to me crying. She said to me, as best as she could through her tears, "You know, Dolly, I will never forget you. I will pray for you and Felix, for your safe return to Holland, and for your well-being, always. I hate to see you go." I also started to cry. This small, gray-haired woman had nursed me, suffered with me, helped me to keep my spirits up during one of the most trying times of my life, and watched over me all these months. We clung to each other. In her hand she clutched the little red book that contained the music from which I played the organ each week. "I want you to have my hymnal book as a memento," she said. "Look inside. I have inscribed it."

I took the book from her and read the following poem that she had written on the first page of *Alexander's Hymns No. 3:*

> *I know not what awaits me,*
> *God kindly veils mine eyes;*
> *And over each step of my onward way*
> *He makes such scenes to rise.*
> *And with every joy He sends me,*
> *comes a sweet and glad surprise.*

> To my little Dutch Dolly, with heaps of love,
> Ethel Morling
> Ipswich, April,1941

At that moment I said a silent prayer for her well-being with the fervent hope that I would never again have to say good-bye to a loved one. Fate, however, would have it differently. We learned that the Dutch soldiers, who had been wounded and were cared for in the hospital, had long since gone home. I was sure that Felix and I were the last survivors of the shipwrecked SS *Simon Bolivar* to return home to my native Holland. We also said a tearful good-bye to Mr. and Mrs. Bland, thanking them profoundly for their care, hospitality, love, and encouragement during these trying months.

We left Ipswich early in the morning of May 2, 1940, for London, where we would board the airplane back to Holland. The Dutch steamship company had arranged for us to stay overnight in a hotel in Folkestone the night before our trip to the airport. It was a beautiful and luxurious hotel where, again, we met some very interesting people at our dinner table. They were quite interested in our story of the shipwreck, our survival, and the months spent recovering from our serious injuries. As we recounted the details, however, we realized that we became quite weary. Obviously, we still were not one hundred percent well. On that last night in England, we retired to our rooms early.

The next morning, May 2 (Felix's birthday), someone from the Dutch Consulate came to take us to the airport in London. When we reached the airport, the plane that would take us home had *Holland* painted in large letters across it. I was so overcome with emotion that I almost fainted. However, that old foreboding feeling, almost like an omen, once again hit me, and I distinctly remember saying, "I'm not going." Felix became upset, and the person from the Dutch Consulate who had driven us to the airport said to me, "There is no other way but to step in."

It turned into a delicate situation, but I had to go. The flight, albeit a short one, was awful and frightening for me. The plane, of course, was small, and the windows were blacked out. There were only a few people on board. I heard planes flying around us, and someone remarked that he hoped they were not German planes. They probably were.

At last we landed safely in Amsterdam, where I fell into the arms of my mother and my other family members. My sister had a large bouquet of flowers for us. What an emotional reunion! There were lots of people waiting at home for us to welcome us back. On that day the festivities in honor of our return well made up for the suffering we endured over the past six months. I was home with my darling mother. And so the first part of our journey through the "Valley of Death" was over.

Back in Holland after the shipwreck

HOLLAND INVADED

Chapter 10: Rotterdam Destroyed

The first two days after we arrived home from England were lively. There was a constant stream of family and friends visiting and bringing food, presents, and clothing for us. They wanted to know every detail about the shipwreck, our recovery, and our six-month stay in England.

My mother did not look well. I found that she had aged; of course, she worried incessantly about us. Now that I was home, I hoped that she would feel better. The Saturday following our return, my mother suggested that we all go to Synagogue to say prayers of thanks for our safe return. There were quite a number of worshippers that day. The Rabbi said a special prayer of thanks, and the Cantor sang special psalms of grace befitting the occasion. At this time I also became closer to Felix's family as a result of all we had been through together.

Several days after our return Felix told me that he was not giving up on his plans to leave Holland and that he had booked the two of us on the SS *Van Rensselaer,* a passenger liner also owned by the Royal Dutch Shipping Company. The ship would sail on May 11, 1940. I did not dare mention this to our families, but Felix's brother Theo was aware of our plans. Theo was a wonderful human being and a rock of support to both of us.

I felt like an ostrich with its head in the sand keeping everything hidden inside of me. "Since we had lost everything," I thought, "I did not own much, so it was better to pack at the last minute." Yet so much had to be done! Felix and I needed new papers, passports, proof of this, proof of that, and it took much time to travel on the bus or the tram to go to the different agencies to acquire the needed paperwork.

The days went by very quickly, and we continued to get a lot of attention from people around us. During this time I wrote to our friends in England to let them know we had arrived safely. But in the midst of our reunions and celebrations, there was no real peace. On the radio we heard that German planes were constantly flying over Holland.

Just as my family made plans to visit my brother in Amersfoort for a short vacation, again terror struck. It was *May 10, 1940.* I was awakened at about four o'clock in the morning by the sound of loud noises and low-flying planes. At first I thought I was dreaming, but then my mother rushed into my room looking white as a sheet. In a stammering voice she said, "Get up and get dressed! It must be the Germans." My sister, who continued to stay with us since my return from England, was awake and also looked quite frightened.

The impossible was happening—war in Holland. It just could not be! Our flat was located near a railroad station, which apparently was one of the first targets of the Germans. We heard bombs exploding all over the city. Neighbors on our street were running in different directions, shouting and gesturing wildly, and appearing not to know what to do next. If you have never experienced low-flying planes and bombings, it is difficult to comprehend how utterly terrifying this is. Not only were we in dire fear for our lives, but the concept of war in Holland was heart-wrenching. Holland was a peace-loving country and had not experienced war in two hundred years.

At seven o'clock in the morning my mother's sister and her youngest son, Jacob (my favorite cousin), came to our door. They both looked weary, frightened, and bewildered. "I want you all to come home with us," my aunt said. The radio was on, and we heard the announcer say that Germany was invading Holland. We were totally shocked to learn that the Germans had also attacked Belgium, Luxembourg, and France on this same day. We had no air raid shelters; it seemed like heads or tails—we'd either survive or be killed. I expected to see Felix next, but we had not heard from him.

My aunt told us that she and her sons would not want to live in a country occupied by Nazis; there was something ominous in the way she spoke. We felt the same. After a short while my aunt went home, leaving us with the serious nature of our thoughts and the indecision of what to do next.

Finally my sister said, "I'm going to Felix's home." My mother still seemed undecided about what to do. I realized that it was difficult for her to leave everything behind. After my sister left, my mother and I gathered up our most important papers and valuable items and set out for Felix's home also. His family lived in Blijdorp, which was a suburb of Rotterdam.

Under normal circumstances, it was a mere twenty-minute walk from our home to Felix's. On this day it took us several hours. We were worried about my sister. The bombings in our city were relentless, and we had to stop and hide each time we heard a bomb. Several times, Dutch soldiers who appeared quite nervous had stopped us and asked for papers, for our nationality, where we were going, who we were. This seemed so absurd to me. We never needed any identification papers in Holland before. But now there was a war going on in my beloved country, and all had changed overnight.

As our long trip to Felix's home progressed, my mother began to look white as a sheet, and I was afraid that something might happen to her. Finally, after what seemed an eternity, we arrived to find Felix's mother, his brother Theo, sister Nellie, and, of course, my sister, Bep (our nickname for Elisabeth). But Felix was not there.

With much anxiety Theo explained that Felix, on his way to our home, had been stopped by Dutch soldiers who had interrogated him about his citizenship. At that time, Felix wore a mustache and an English raincoat that made him look typically German. Now the Dutch soldiers had received orders to intern all foreign subjects.

Felix's family had somehow received word that Felix, along with many other aliens, had been interned in De Doelen, a large concert hall in the center of Rotterdam (the Coolsingel). Upon seeing our worried faces, Theo explained in a sorrowful voice that the Dutch police were taking all aliens to their headquarters to which they were required to report. All of us were very upset yet continued to expect Felix to walk through the door at any moment. I thought to myself, "Had we gone through that six-month ordeal that is finally behind us only to be separated or killed?" Felix's mother was fervently Orthodox and always had her prayer book with her. She went into another room in the house and we all knew she was praying very hard for her son.

A few days went by. We were in agony. We could see Rotterdam burning and could even smell the smoke. Still, no Felix. We heard on the radio that the Hague had been hit, that the Germans had ruined a great deal of the west coast, and thousands of people in Rotterdam had lost their lives. We also heard that Belgium and Luxembourg, as well as France, had all been attacked on that tragic day of May 10, 1940. Belgium, Luxembourg and my country, the Netherlands, surrendered after five days of relentless bombing and destruction. France had held out against the Germans for about three weeks but capitulated beginning June, 1940. In our minds it was already the end of the world.

Three days went by, four days, and still no sign of Felix. Looking at Felix's mother, I could tell that she was desperate, but outwardly she tried to appear calm. On the fifth day of the bombing, the radio announcer told listeners that the Dutch had capitulated and the queen and her children had fled the country. I vividly remember how this announcement threw me into emotional shock. Both events—Felix lost somewhere, and our queen fleeing—had a devastating effect on my nerves. It was a deep feeling of abandonment. Felix's words came back to me, words I had not believed, "I assure you that Hitler is not afraid of your queen." I hoped that they were just rumors.

Finally, after what seemed like an eternity of bombing, burning, killing, and merciless destruction of the city of Rotterdam, the German troops marched in. The city was a sea of fire—Dante's hell. But that did not deter the Germans. Stepping over the dead and wounded, they marched on singing "Gloria Victoria." This was the proud, so-called master race that the Dutch had to put up with for many years to come.

The German soldiers also marched into Blijdorp and onto our street. We had been sitting on the stairs for the past five days to protect ourselves from the bombing. Suddenly there was a sharp knocking at the door. Panic ensued; it was a German soldier. We didn't know what to do.

The knocking continued. My sister got up, kissed, and hugged everyone, and said, crying bitterly, "Until I see you all in the hereafter."

Finally, Nellie went to the door and opened it a crack. The German soldier told her that the troops needed pots, pans, utensils, and other items. We could hear her speak in German to the soldier, and she gave him what he had asked for. Then we saw more soldiers going to neighbors on the street, and loading up on different items from their homes.

Some hours later, Theo said to us, "Listen, I'm going to find out what happened to Felix." Felix's mother turned white but did not hold him back. Theo never thought of his own danger in anything he did for others. A long time went by, and the house was full of tension. Finally, after many hours, another miracle occurred: both Theo and Felix walked through the door. In an unbelievable set of circumstances, Theo found Felix wandering about the city. Felix looked terrible. He was unshaven, unwashed, quite thin, and his coat was almost in rags. But thank goodness, we had him back with us. As we hovered around him, he told us what had happened to him over the past several days.

The bombs had destroyed the concert hall where he and other foreigners had been interned. After the guard fled, he and several others fled also. On his way back home several Dutch soldiers had halted him and took him to the cellar of a home, where he was locked up with other people who turned out to be escapees from the local jail.

At this point Felix was still in the hands of the Dutch. After the capitulation, the Germans had taken over the homes where they heard people in the cellar. Felix told the other men to be still. He yelled in German that there were German people locked up. A German officer opened the cellar door and detained all of them. Felix and the others had to walk along for hours with the German troops over De Maasbrug, located in the southern part of the city where everything was burning. It looked like a place of slaughter.

The Germans then seized what had been a school, detained the men in the building, and announced that all men would be deported to Germany. Felix approached a high-ranking officer and told him that he was German and did not belong in this place. The first officer did not respond to him, and neither did the second. Finally, toward morning, a third officer listened to him and let him go.

Was it a guardian angel again who watched over him and protected him? All of us said prayers of thanks, and Felix's mother prepared and served a good meal. Afterwards, Felix cleaned up, and soon friends and neighbors stopped by. The conversation went on late into the evening.

We were still alive, all of us together, and the next step was to find out where my aunt, uncle, and cousins were and how our friends had fared during that terrible week. Here again, God had been with us, and though we did not know what the future would bring, we could extract some hope from the events—and the survival—of our recent past.

Chapter 11: The Cruel Beginnings

My mother, sister, and I stayed on for a few days at the home of Felix and his family who lived in a more secure area in the suburbs. A few days later, we learned that the queen had officially left Holland. All of us were devastated upon hearing the disappointing news. We felt lost and abandoned. My mother said, "We cannot stay here forever. We must go home and see what has happened."

I cannot describe the complete chaos we discovered on our way home; we realized it had been a miracle that we had not been killed by the bombs. From what we saw on the streets, entire neighborhoods were completely destroyed. German soldiers were everywhere. Dutch soldiers were led at gunpoint by the Germans to be deported. Dead bodies were strewn all over the streets.

Although the railroad station had been badly damaged, we found our flat in the same condition as we had left it. Our neighbors came to our home right away. We were in shock—our small, beautiful country had been taken by surprise. Since we knew that Hitler had invaded Denmark and Norway in April it would have been smart to stay in England, but as I mentioned before, the British did not allow any German nationals to remain in England.

With a very serious, almost despondent look on her face, my mother said to my sister and me, "We know what it will be like for Jewish people under a German regime; we must get some valuables together and bring them to the neighbors." She immediately began to gather photographs—from our youth, from our school days, of our grandparents, and of other family members. In later years, I realized that this had been a brilliant move on my mother's part.

The next day we packed up three large suitcases, just in case. But in case of what? What would our future hold? At least we still had each other. We had word that my brother and his wife in Amersfoort were fine, but we had no word of my brother Ben. No one knew of his whereabouts.

The day we packed our suitcases, my sister said, "We have not heard from Aunt Sien and the family; we must go there and find out how they are." My aunt lived not far from us; so later in the day the three of us walked to their home to find it was still standing. But where were they? Panic set in and we were very worried about their welfare. After making many telephone calls and talking to mutual friends, we learned the terrible news that my aunt, uncle, and their two sons had all tried to commit suicide, as did so many others who preferred death to torture when the Germans marched into the city. They had taken a lethal dose of morphine that they had obtained from a pharmacist friend. All became violently ill. My twenty-six-year-old cousin, Maurits, had died. Jacob, the younger brother, and my uncle, the brilliant chessmaster, survived the attempt. My poor aunt, however, suffered a stroke and was in a nearby hospital. The pharmacist survived. She was later deported and died in a concentration camp.

My Aunt Sien, Felix, me, and my cousin Jacob before our departure

My cousin Maurits de Haas

The oldest son, Simon, lived in Amsterdam and had escaped this ordeal. We wondered if things would have turned out differently had Simon been with his family. He had a way of dealing with difficult situations, and perhaps he would have talked them out of choosing to end their lives.

When we arrived at the hospital to see my aunt, we found her in a frightful condition. Her face and arms were covered with yellow spots that looked like burn marks. The nurse on duty explained that an assistant, in an attempt to revive my poor aunt, had put hot water bottles on her body—which turned out to be too hot. Because of the stroke my aunt was unable to communicate this to the assistant and ended up with burn marks all over her body. As gently as possible, we tried to explain to my aunt the fate of her son, Maurits. We had the feeling that somehow she already knew. Maurits had been a handsome, most intelligent young man with a bright future ahead of him—a future destroyed by the Germans who invaded our country. My uncle was slowly recovering after his suicide attempt. It was a very traumatic situation for my family, but we all coped the best way we could.

The next day the funeral of my cousin, Maurits, took place at a Jewish cemetery, *Het Toepad,* which was located east of Rotterdam. My sister and I, as well as friends and neighbors, attended. The Rabbi of Rotterdam conducted the somber event. I remember that every word the Rabbi spoke was like a pearl of wisdom. In a simple wooden coffin my cousin was laid to rest, and we all recited Kaddish, the prayer for departed loved ones. This prayer confirms our faith in God and does not include complaints of our adversities.

During this hour of grief, I could only think of the overwhelming confusion. I kept staring at the words on the gate at the entrance of the cemetery that read, "He who is born must die; He who dies enters life eternal." I tried to contemplate these words and make some sense out of what had happened, but it did not help much.

We had to bike to the cemetery, which was many miles away from Rotterdam. After the funeral we were physically and emotionally exhausted from everything. At home that night we turned on the radio and learned, much to our consternation, that many prominent intellectuals in Holland had taken their lives as well. They knew what a Nazi regime would entail—concentration camps and persecutions. They too had chosen death over torture.

The weeks following the invasion were marked with the typical German characteristics of diplomatic "double-talk." Right after the military settled in the SS followed, and the Dutch newspapers were subjected to censorship. Over the next several days we read bold headlines in the newspapers announcing that Hitler had appointed Dr. Arthur Seyss-Inquart as head of the German occupation forces in Holland. Seyss-Inquart was an Austrian lawyer who had betrayed his own country to Hitler. Seyss-Inquart was an odd name for our Dutch language, and secretly we often made up puns.

Seyss-Inquart was a fanatical Nazi and a staunch follower of Hitler's orders. In the short time that the Germans were in our country, they had seized many government buildings. It was bizarre to the Dutch when the newspapers announced that Seyss-Inquart was to present a speech in the famous Ridderzaal (Knight's Hall) in the Hague, the beautiful place where our queen always presented her yearly "Troonrede" (loosely translated, State of the Union speech). This event was always celebrated with much joy and festivities in the month of September (Prinsjesdag). We did not feel this festive spirit in the anticipation of Seyss-Inquart's speech. He spoke about a master race, the Aryan race, "Arbeit macht frei" (work gives freedom), the victory of the Germans, and how Germany had won for Europe. He also vowed to get rid of the Jews. We turned the radio on and off, but it seemed as if this speech lasted forever. That night I found that I hated the German language. It seemed harsh and distasteful to me.

We had a number of collaborators in Holland, called the "Nationaal Socialistische Beweging," or the NSB. The most notorious of them was a man named Mussert, a civil engineer. The NSB helped the Germans to familiarize themselves with the customs and culture of my country. In addition to all of the atrocities was the humiliation that the Germans referred to our country as "The Westland," or the "Western Province of Germany."

Soon the Nazis started to evoke shameless insinuations on the Jews. For instance, they showed a film to both the Nazis and the members of the NSB called *Der Ewige Jude,* meaning "The Eternal Jew." The film depicted Jewish people as rats. This was only the beginning. These events had a most nerve-wracking effect on the Jewish population. We began to panic.

My sister had gone back to live with the family for whom she worked in the countryside. We were grateful that my oldest brother, Ies, and his wife in Amersfoort were in satisfactory condition considering the circumstances. But we were extremely concerned about my brother Ben. We did not know where he was or if he was all right. My mother had become the strong one now. I leaned on her for strength and reassurance. I remember she said to me, "You have to be strong; we will get through this somehow." Little did she know—little did any of us know at the time—the fate that would befall us. She continued, "I have confidence in Ben; he knows what he is doing." We knew that Ben had many friends in Belgium and in England, but we could not begin to imagine what had happened to him.

Our neighbors and non-Jewish friends were marvelous. They visited our home often and would try to say comforting things like "Don't take things literally. Anti-Semitism is built into the German system." Or they would try to console us with the reassurance that "this is just Nazi-politics; don't take it so hard."

Many Christian citizens protested heavily against the hatred the Germans invoked against the Jews, but the Germans were stirred up by Hitler to such an extent that they began to also threaten the Gentiles—especially the Catholics because Hitler believed that Catholicism was a part of Judaism. The Germans tried to cause a wide rift between Christians and their Jewish friends.

It is very difficult for me to write down the exact succession of unspeakably insane measures that the Nazis imposed upon the Jewish people. For awhile, all regulations regarding Jews appeared in the newspapers. Later, after they found out where Jewish people lived, the Nazis issued all orders in writing, delivered to the homes of Jews.

One of the first orders to appear in the newspaper read as follows:

All Jews, living on the coast since 1936, must leave their residences immediately.

This included Felix's mother, his sister Nellie, and all refugees from Germany, Poland, and Austria who came to Holland after 1936. But where would they go? Felix's mother had just begun to settle in, and now we had to tell her that she must move again. It was heartbreaking to watch her cry bitterly when we told her; she just couldn't comprehend why.

I had not felt close to Felix's mother and sister. There was something I couldn't put my finger on. First I considered the language and cultural barriers. I also considered the German custom that the older daughter should have the pleasure of male company before the younger son had a girlfriend; could there have been jealousy? After the war, I credited myself with saving all of their lives by taking them to Amersfoort. But at this time, we all tried the best we could to overlook our differences and try to help each other.

During the time we learned that Felix's family would have to move, I suddenly got an idea and optimistically blurted out, "Let's take them to Amersfoort!" At this, Felix's mother began to cry. In between her sobs she asked, "Where is Amersfoort? Where can we go? We don't know anyone in Amersfoort."

We patiently told her of my family in Amersfoort—my beloved Aunt Flora, after whom I was named, and my uncle, Jules Frank. They had lived there ever since they had married. My Aunt Flora was a warm and compassionate woman, filled with love for others, and always eager to help. Her husband, Uncle Jules, was a dignified man, dedicated to the tenets of the Jewish religion and a prominent figure on the board of the local Synagogue. Felix's mother and sister reluctantly packed some suitcases, and later that week we hired a taxi. My mother and I accompanied them to Amersfoort, where my family warmly welcomed them.

Though it was nice to be together with my family again and to see my brother and sister-in-law, it was difficult to fake a festive mood. My aunt and uncle lived in a small but lovely home surrounded by canals and other natural beauty. Whenever we came to their home, a sense of peace and warmth came over us. I have never forgotten the street where they harmoniously lived for many years, Joannes van Dieststraat No. 13. I remember that they had a pet chicken named Jansje, which had the run of the house and often dominated the family.

But of course this trip to their home did not produce the same sense of peacefulness because now we saw things with different eyes. I felt that Felix's mother was not comprehending everything, and in a sense I thought that was good. After all, Holland, for her, was still a strange country, and the language was difficult to understand. We tried to keep her from listening to the radio, where all day long Germans boasted of their victories or berated the Jews, who they said would soon be eradicated. The two brothers, Theo and Felix, took the time to find a place for Nellie and their mother. This was easy enough it turned out. Within a

Amersfoort

few days they had located a furnished home on a nice street in Amersfoort, called the Rubensstraat.

After everyone was settled, Theo, Felix, my mother, and I went back to Rotterdam. Theo and Felix resumed their positions in the offices of their grain business. For a while life seemed to have calmed down, but we still held onto our disgust and fear of the Germans, who were taking possession of our country. During this time, the SS and the Gestapo had rooted themselves in Holland. The stolid expressions on their faces and the power they wielded predicted what the future would hold for the Jews.

It was about this time that, for reasons unexplained until the time of this writing, I began to cut out and save newspaper articles concerning Jews. I hid these clippings deep in my closet where my mother would not find them.

I was thinking of going back to the Royal Music Conservatory where I had studied music before my ill-fated trip on the SS *Simon Bolivar.* But when I arrived there, the Dutch flag had already been replaced by the Nazi flag, and the Royal Dutch Music Conservatory had been reduced to the "Music Conservatory."

My Aunt Sien was able to go home but remained crippled. All of us lived in fear and panic. We tried frantically to obtain visas for other countries, which was just about unthinkable because of what Hitler's Blitzkrieg had already done in Europe.

The real terror began in September 1940, followed by almost five years of unspeakable atrocities and crimes of torment for the Jewish population. This was the true beginning of living in "The Valley of Death."

Chapter 12: The Persecutions Begin

The month of September, 1940, began with a series of unending ordinances directed at the Jews. They were called, in Dutch, "Bekendmaking Voor Joden" (loosely translated, Summons for Jews). They always ended with the following:

ALL JEWS WHO DO NOT ADHERE TO THESE SUMMONS WILL BE ARRESTED AND SENT TO THE CONCENTRATION CAMP IN MAUTHAUSEN.

I remember the first order, or summons, was that every Jew had to report to the local district locale (the name and address of the locale was then stipulated in the ordinance) to sign important papers to indicate whether they were fully Jewish, half-Jewish, or one-quarter Jewish; how far back their Jewish ancestry could be traced; how many grandparents from either side of the family were Jewish, and so on. We were even asked about the ethnicity of our great-grandparents. If a Christian man was married to a Jewish woman, or vice versa, there was talk of sterilization.

The Nazis were insanely preoccupied with these kinds of matters because they were obsessed with keeping the Aryan race free of any Jewish blood. And like frightened sheep, we all followed each other to obey these bizarre ordinances.

Shortly after this particular summons, another one appeared in the papers. It ordered all Jews to appear at a certain place to have their photograph taken. The instructions read: "The left ear has to be exposed; women, no earrings, hair combed back." With much sadness in our hearts we obeyed the ordinance. A German took our photograph, then attached it to a booklet stamped with a *J* for Jew (Jood in Dutch). The Germans, in their twisted minds, thought that the names "Sara" and "Israel" were uniquely Jewish, so in each booklet, the name "Sara" was printed before each woman's first name, and "Israel" before each man's first name. This document was called, in Dutch, *Persoonsbewijs*, meaning "identification certificate." We had to carry this with us at all times.

There was an area in Amsterdam called "The Jordaan" where many working-class Jews lived harmoniously with non-Jewish working-class people. I don't know where this name came from, but because of my interest in languages, I always assumed it was derived from the River Jordan.

Many people from East European countries lived in The Jordaan and so the Dutch language became mixed with Jiddish expressions. Jiddish is a mixture of Hebrew, German, and Polish. For example, Amsterdam was lovingly called Mokum, from the Hebrew word *makum*, meaning "city" or "place." Many Jiddish words and expressions became, in some cases, the etymology of the Dutch language, at least in this particular part of Amsterdam. For instance, people would refer to the jail as *bajis* (from the Hebrew *bajit*, meaning "house"). *Jatten* was the expression for stealing; it came from the Hebrew word *jad*, meaning "hand." A funny and popular Dutch song about courageous boys even had some Jiddish words in it; for example, "*tov* boys"— *tov* from the Hebrew, meaning "good."

The Nazis did not like the close relationships between Jews and Gentiles in The Jordaan, so they often instigated riots by heckling the Jewish people. This heckling led to a terrible revolt by the Gentiles against the Nazis. The Christian population began to strike in Amsterdam and surrounding areas. People stopped going to work in factories, retail stores, and other places of work. These people were necessary for the Germans to support their war machine, and now everything stood still. The strike took place around February 25, 1941; as we understood it, this was the first protest against one of the most powerful enemy occupations in history.

The Dutch did not give up easily, but they were powerless against the Germans. When the Germans began capturing and killing Jews, the non-Jewish strikers screamed, "We want our Jews; leave our Jews alone!" Hundreds of Christian protesters were killed during this strike, which lasted several days. This event of the Nazi occupation in Holland is written in blood. We must forever remember the moral courage of the non-Jewish people in Holland.

In the meantime, the English began to attack the Germans, and so we had English and German fighter planes waging a war over our heads. There were continuous air raids. During this time the Germans initiated a crafty plan. They appointed a body of prominent Jewish people in Amsterdam, which they called *De Joodse Raad*, meaning "the Jewish Council." It was headed by the industrialist Mr. A. Asscher and by Professor Dr. D. Cohen. The Germans promised these members of the Jewish Council that they would be in charge of all Dutch Jewish affairs in Holland in connection with Nazi ordinances! At least that's what they were told—and it is what they naively believed. Now, all heinous actions by the occupying forces quickly followed one after the other. The Jewish Council had the dubious task of urging all Jewish people to register with them in Amsterdam thinking that they could trust the Germans if they cooperated with them.

One day at the beginning of 1941, my mother said to me, "Why don't you go to the zoo to get your mind off things." We had been members of the Rotterdam Zoo for as long as we had lived there, and it was not far from our home. I was always exceptionally fond of animals, so I was elated to learn that the zoo had been restored and reopened after the invasion. I became enthusiastic, so I got my bike and rode to the Rotterdam Zoo. When I arrived, I parked my bike in the bike rack and walked over to the entrance.

To my great disgust I came upon a large sign with bold lettering that stated *Voor Joden Verboden*. This means "forbidden for Jews." I must have stood there for a long, long time reading and rereading the sign. I was abhorred; it was like a knife through my heart. For a moment I thought, "I will go in anyway; what do those animals know?" But I remembered the dreaded document, stamped with the letter *J* deep in my pocket. I dared not go in.

After this demeaning experience I rode my bike to my aunt and uncle's home to see how they were doing. My aunt was still under medical care, and she looked miserable. But at least she was home and could move around a bit. My favorite cousin, Jacob, and my uncle were also home. My uncle had never been a big talker, but after I had told him what had happened at the zoo, he said, "Prepare yourself, this is just the beginning. No good can be expected."

After my visit I rode home. I kept myself occupied with cutting out all of the ordinances that appeared in the newspapers. I hid them in my closet and cried. My mother asked me, "Whatever are you always cutting out?" Because I did not want to upset her, I ignored her question and changed the subject. During this time the canals were frozen. I loved ice skating, and so I spent many a day skating.

Felix and his brother were still able to work in their office, which had been relocated to Hillegersberg, a suburb of Rotterdam, because the Coolsingel office in the center of the city had been burned down during the invasion. Our evenings were usually spent together with our families.

Signs reading "Forbidden for Jews" began to appear all over. Jews were no longer allowed in parks, theaters, or schools. These dreaded signs were everywhere in the summer of 1941. In front of the home where the famous painter Rembrandt Van Rijn had lived in Amsterdam was a sign that read "Jews Are Forbidden Here!" Jews were not even allowed in the center of Amsterdam. In addition, the Germans mandated a separation between Jews and non-Jews: it was absolutely forbidden for the Jewish population to mingle with Christians.

In this year, 1941, many Jewish couples began to leave their babies on the doorsteps of Christian homes, churches, and convents. But the Germans immediately stopped this by putting bold ordinances in the newspapers, stating the following:

ALL CHILDREN AND BABIES LEFT OR FOUND AT DOORSTEPS OF NON-JEWISH HOMES AND CHURCHES ARE DECLARED JEWISH AND WILL BE SENT TO MAUTHAUSEN.

The Jewish Council was completely misled into believing that they could help their own. In our Dutch way of thinking, it was unbelievable that we were to be put in concentration camps. Many families preferred death over living with this prospect.

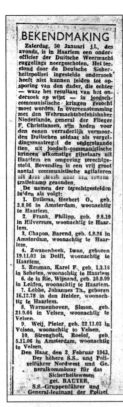

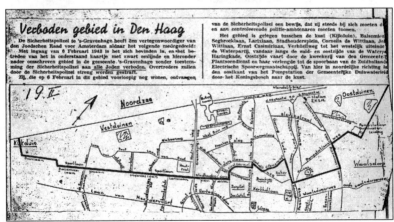

Top left: The Germans were very proud to annouce the executions of innocent Dutch citizens of the resistance whom they labeled "Communists"
Top right: New regulations restricting mailing privileges for the Jews
Below: Map of the areas where Jews were allowed, and not allowed, to be

For as long as I can remember, there was a Jewish weekly newspaper in Holland called *Het Nieuw Israelitiesch Weekblad*. In 1941, this newspaper was banned by the Germans and replaced by another, called the *Jewish Weekly*, which was nothing more than a vehicle in which the Germans printed their regulations and ordinances. Soon, Jews had to turn in their radios and bicycles, and they were not allowed to have telephones in their homes. They were absolutely forbidden to enter the homes of non-Jewish people.

At that time I had not heard of Mauthausen. I looked it up in my atlas and found that it was located somewhere in Austria. At first—as I understood it—it served as a concentration camp for anti-Nazis; later it was the camp most dreaded by the Dutch Jewish people. Mauthausen was supposed to be a labor camp under the most atrocious conditions. People who had the unfortunate fate to end up there never came back, whether they were Jews or non-Jews. It is said that the commander of this camp, Franz Ziereis, gave his son fifty Jews for his birthday for target shooting practice.

We still lived in our flat in Rotterdam, though we could not communicate with the family. There was danger everywhere. One day, my Uncle Saam came to our home unexpectedly. He had walked all the way from his home to ours. He had aged drastically, almost before my eyes! Instead of the tall, handsome, impressive man that I remembered, I saw a shrunken old gentleman with a face full of sorrow. He said, "I want to know, first of all, how you both are doing, and then I have to tell you something important."

We talked a bit, and of course the conversation focused on what was happening to the Jewish population. Although my father's side of the family had not been very religious, they all knew they were Jewish. My uncle said, looking at no one in particular, "You see, things are getting worse and worse for the Jews; don't you see we have reached the point of no return? I discussed the whole situation with Aunt Sophie and the girls, and we have decided to convert to Christianity, you see. If we become Christians, you see, we might not fall prey to the Germans." My mother and I could not believe what we were hearing. He continued, "We have dear friends in the Christian community, you see, and we are going to convert to Catholicism."

My mother, moderate as she always was, said nothing. But I said, "But uncle, what about your name Cohen; it sounds pretty Jewish." I could see that he had anticipated our reaction, but he said, "I feel it is my duty to do everything possible to save our lives." There was silence for a long time and I expected him to advise us to do the same thing. But that did not happen. Finally, my mother broke the silence and said, "Well, I really wish and hope that it is for your good."

In my ignorance I said, "How does that work? Do you now have to wear a cross?" But my uncle did not go into details. He said to us, "Sophie and the girls wish you good luck; you see, maybe the war will be over soon." In my youthful imagination, I pictured my aunt and uncle kneeling in a church and making the sign of the cross; I figured that they had to do something about the last name of Cohen. My mother said, "We are living in such a bizarre time, nothing surprises me anymore. Let's wish them good luck and forget about it."

That night in bed, I kept thinking about our lives and especially how my uncle's decision would work out. I had been very close with my Cousin Lenie, my aunt and uncle's youngest daughter, and wondered what her fate would be with her new religion. After the war I learned that my aunt, uncle, their oldest daughter and her husband all perished at the hands of the Nazis. Their two grandchildren survived. My cousin, with whom I was close, survived in a convent. She remained a Catholic.

WHAT GENES DO THE GERMANS HAVE?

Chapter 13: The Tyrant's Lash

The High Holy Days in the fall of 1940 had come and gone by without, of course, the usual feeling of solemnity. My mother bravely walked to the local Synagogue on the day of Rosh Hashanah, but I preferred to stay home. I only accompanied my mother on the Day of Atonement, the Yom Kippur Holy Day. It was a long distance to walk from our home to the Synagogue with the inevitable encounter of German soldiers, who were up to no good. I thought it ludicrous to go to the Temple, but I went for the sake of my mother.

The festivals following the High Holy Days—Sukkot, Simchat Torah, and Hanukkah—normally such happy days, were spent at home. I kept thinking with nostalgia about the festival of Sukkot, so-called to remind us of the Jews' exodus out of Egypt. This holiday is also known as the Harvest Festival when we, as students of the Hebrew School, went on trips with our teachers and other adults to the forests to gather the lush purple heather for the decorations in our Sukkah.

But during this time, these holidays were filled with anxiety and fear. My mother tried to retain some semblance of the way we celebrated Friday night Shabbat in the past. She would place a white tablecloth on our table, prepare some special dishes, and attempt to put on a happy face, saying to us, "Let's say a prayer." The ritual always ended with Kaddish.

Often, looking at the three suitcases we had packed "in case of," I said to my mother, "I wonder if the prayers will do any good." My mother would reply, "The war will be over soon." Alone in bed at night, I would hold a monologue with God, who now, in my mind, had become a stranger, someone who did not care any longer, someone who had abandoned us. It was very confusing for me.

One day, in the spring of 1941, an ordinance appeared in the newspaper stating that all Jews still living on the shoreline had to leave their homes immediately. We were to leave our pets behind. We were to pick up maps to see which cities were affected by this ordinance. Rotterdam, of course, was affected; it was the largest and most important harbor in Europe, if not the world.

But where to? Amersfoort, of course, the most significant town in our lives. We immediately got in touch with my aunt, uncle, and cousins in Rotterdam, who also were at their wit's end. They told us that friends had offered them a place to stay for the time being. Some friends within Felix's circle of acquaintances had suggested that we go into hiding. But how could we go into hiding in Holland, a small country, as flat as a pancake?

The Jewish people in Holland were further threatened by the German authorities to leave everything behind and turn in house keys to a particular German office. Pets would be destroyed. If these orders were not followed by a certain date, transgressors would be arrested and sent to Mauthausen. And so, our three "in case of" suitcases became useful, after all.

So many things happened in 1940 that it would require the pages of ten books to record everything. Our situation could be compared to a revolving door: if one could not get out, the evils went on and on and on. Felix, whom we saw regularly, kept saying, "We must do everything and try to get visas and get out."

Jewish people had to turn in their radios in April of 1941. In one respect, we were glad that we no longer had to listen to the blarings of Seyss-Inquart, Rauter, and Aus der Funten, who assured the Dutch population in their speeches that they would soon get rid of the Jews.

The Germans had already begun to confiscate all Jewish businesses and corporations. They simply sent out letters notifying the owners and presidents of these companies that their businesses were now in the hands of a German *Verwalter,* meaning "manager" or "administrator." The

German administrator would come; seize all books, papers, bank deposits, and other important information; then promptly fire all Dutch employees. Among the hundreds of newspaper clippings and documents that I hid during those years was the following letter of dismissal sent to Felix by the German *Verwalter:*

REGISTERED LETTER

In regards to ordinance #198 by the High Commissioner of the occupied Dutch territories, I have been ordered to inform you that you have been dismissed from your position with the N.V. Nidera Handelscompagnie, Rotterdam, as of immediately. Please acknowledge receipt of this letter. On behalf of the High Commissioner of the occupied Dutch territory, Dr. Arthur Seyss-Inquart.

Felix and his brother Theo had to stay in Rotterdam for a while because they were required to "assist" in liquidating the company and show the German administrator "the ropes."

My mother and I packed a few more items, and I made sure that I took all of my newspaper clippings with me to Amersfoort. We had a cat named Mimi, which we gave to our neighbors who assured us that they would take good care of her. Valuable items such as paintings, silver, flatware, china, and anything that was too heavy to carry had to be left behind. The Germans would then have access to our precious belongings.

Of course, we were welcomed with open arms by my brother and his wife, as well as our other family members. But all of us felt aimless and hopeless because we now ventured through a labyrinth of hell that we could not understand. We had lost contact with our family in Rotterdam; everyone was going in different directions not knowing what to do. We all knew that a disaster would follow, an unknown but terrible fate, an Armageddon.

It so happened that my brother, Ies, had Christian friends who owned a bookstore. The owner was ill; his wife was also ailing. Upon hearing of our fate, this couple immediately offered my mother and me the entire second floor of their property, fully furnished, free of rent, in exchange for help in their bookstore.

The arrangement worked out well, but we felt guilty living there because we were not supposed to mingle with non-Jewish people. We also noticed that these good people were not aware of—or perhaps did not pay attention to—the endless ordinances and regulations that frequently appeared in the newspapers.

One day a German officer came into the bookstore and looked around. He then turned to me and said that we had to make sure that no books by Jewish authors were carried in the store any longer. He was so engrossed in the orders from his superior that he repeated himself over and over again. Thank goodness he never asked me to produce my papers! Inwardly, I was shaken terribly. He left, clicking his heels. It was such an awful experience for me that I had to discuss this situation with the owner, telling him that I could no longer work in his bookstore. He and his wife felt very sorry about this because the arrangement had been working out so well for all of us. Consequently, my mother and I had to look for another place to live.

We were able to find a small but neatly furnished place on the same street where Nellie, Felix's sister, and her mother lived in the Rubensstraat. After Felix and Theo "assisted" the German administrator in liquidating the family business, they too moved in with their mother and sister. And so, for the time being our families found some consolation in each other's company.

Every regulation from the Germans was, of course, a threat and was intended to produce a vicious cycle of problems for the Jewish people. We could not live a normal life. For example, after taking away businesses from Jews, the Germans issued a new ordinance stating that Jews who were unemployed would be sent to camps to work for the Germans.

In Amersfoort, I remember there was a very courageous mayor who refused to put up signs that read "Jews Not Allowed." He also removed signs that the Germans had already put up. But soon this brave mayor was replaced by an NSB mayor.

N.V. NIDERA HANDELSCOMPAGNIE
ROTTERDAM

TELEGRAM-ADRES: „ALFREKO"

TELEFOON No. 44291
POSTREKENING: 57980

TIJDELIJK ADRES:
ALYDA VAN SPANGENSINGEL 17
HILLEGERSBERG
POSTBOX 678, ROTTERDAM

HILLEGERSBERG, 11.November 1941
BIJ ROTTERDAM

Einschreiben.

Herrn F.Levi,
23 Rubensstraat
Amersfoort.

Laut Verordnung 198 des Reichskommissars fuer die besetzten niederländischen Gebiete habe ich die Verpflichtung Ihnen Ihre Stellung bei obiger Firma zu kündigen zum 28.Februar 1942.

An diesem Tage erfolgt die Auszahlung einer Abfindung gemäss den Anordnungen des Herrn Reichskommissars fuer die besetzten niederländischen Gebiete.

Ich bitte Sie mir den Empfang dieses Schreibens zu bestätigen.

Hochachtungsvoll
N.V.Nidera Handelscompagnie

Treuhänder.

Above: The newspaper article stating radios had to be turned in
Below: Letter to Felix to relinquish the business

One evening my brother and I attended a concert in the music hall in Amersfoort when suddenly, upon orders of the local German commandant, we heard a voice over the loudspeaker ordering all Jews in attendance to leave immediately. Every person in the concert hall that evening left in solidarity with their Jewish countrymen.

The following Jewish professionals were no longer allowed to work: attorneys, doctors, pharmacists, notaries, and midwives, along with a host of other highly trained professionals. Jewish people were no longer allowed to go to public places such as parks, hotels, restaurants, swimming pools, concert halls, libraries, and museums. No Jew could continue to be a member of a tennis club, football team, bridge team, or even a group of fishing buddies. We could not even enter beauty parlors or barber shops any longer.

The Jewish community in Amersfoort had always been close with the non-Jewish community. But now, with one ordinance, this was all over.

Chapter 14: Through the Eye of a Needle

The non-Jewish population was, of course, also suffering at the hands of the Nazis. They too had to follow all kinds of absurd regulations, which were always accompanied by threats.

For example, schools were no longer allowed to teach students about world history, particularly World War I, which the Germans had lost. In addition, anything pertaining to the royal family was strictly forbidden to appear in textbooks. Photographs of Queen Wilhelmina, her daughter Princess Juliana, Juliana's husband Prince Bernhard, or their children were not allowed to be seen anywhere—all pictures were to be destroyed. Indications that there ever was a royal family in Holland were forbidden.

One would have thought that the Germans had plenty of other things to contend with. But I do believe that their power was laced with sadistic tendencies, and they took great pleasure in evil acts against citizens. Teachers were ordered, with many threats, to carry out these ordinances. Ironically, these orders produced just the opposite: by drawing attention to these changes, the history of Holland and information about the Royal House of Nassau was reinforced. We knew anyway that Queen Wilhelmina was in England, and that the princess and her children were in Canada.

Even streets that had been named after the Royal House had to be changed, and streets named after Jewish painters, writers, scientists, and other prominent people were eliminated altogether. Holland was robbed of honoring those who had contributed much to its culture and history.

Food also became scarce because the Germans took away anything they could get their hands on, "upon orders of the Führer." They stole works of art, clothing, shoes, and other goods and sent everything to their Heimat, their homes in Germany. They looted constantly. If the Germans did not want the Dutch to see what they were doing, they simply placed signs up that read

PEOPLE WILL BE SHOT HERE WITHOUT WARNING.

The floor that my family and I occupied on the Rubensstraat was owned by a young couple who had two small children. They were very nice, patriotic people and allowed us to use their telephone and other facilities. The husband, Jan, was involved with one of the Resistance Movements that had sprung up shortly after the German invasion. He had a crystal radio on which he could listen to the BBC, the *Voice of the Free World*. At night we would come together and learn what really went on. Queen Wilhelmina, now in exile in England, spoke often on this radio program and sent encouraging words of hope to her former subjects in Holland to remain steadfast (Je Maintiendrai).

The citizens who joined these Resistance Movements were people of great courage. They were not afraid to take risks for their own lives or for the lives of their families. We learned during the course of the war that great numbers of patriots had been killed by the Nazis. When we lived on the Rubensstraat, we did not know that Jan, our brave landlord and good friend, would be among them. How sorrowful and full of grief these years were.

At that time we were not familiar with the operations of the Resistance Movements, but Jan told us all they had accomplished. Thanks to the bravery of people in the resistance, bridges, railroads, and other important transportation and communications that were of value to the German war machine were destroyed or made unusable for the Germans.

One outstanding underground newspaper was called *Het Parool*, meaning "Word of Honor" (translated from the Dutch). People who wrote for this newspaper would play an important role—if not the most important—in our lives during those desperate years.

During the time we lived with the young couple, we would learn of events that would never be written about in the Nazi-controlled newspapers. Jan brought us newspapers printed by the Resistance Movements in which their articles urged the Jewish people not to obey orders from the Germans. It was also strange to read in these resistance papers that we should ignore orders from the Jewish Council. The Jewish Council continued to urge the Jewish population to come and register their addresses.

Of course, the vast majority of Jewish people believed in and followed orders from the Jewish Council because they were convinced that they knew what was best for us. Felix, however, believed that the council advisors were a bunch of ignorant people and that the organization was mixed with stupidity and blindness from the true purposes of the Nazis in whose hands the Jewish Council played. It turned out later that Felix was right. For example, there was a well-known bank in Amsterdam called Lippmann-Rosenthal, originally owned by German Jews. The bank, of course, had been taken over by the Nazis; however, they kept the name of the bank the same to fool the Jewish people into thinking that it was still run by Jewish business people.

One day, the following ordinance appeared in the newspapers:

ALL ITEMS OF GOLD, SUCH AS GOLD COINS, JEW-
ELRY, OR ANY OTHER ARTICLES OF GOLD OR
ANTIQUES MUST BE TURNED IN BY JEWS TO THE
LIPPMANN-ROSENTHAL BANK IN AMSTERDAM.

The ordinance stated a deadline for turning in these items as well as the address of the bank. Felix's brother Theo, who was gullible, immediately went to Amsterdam and turned in all of his gold coins and other valuables. Felix and I, of course, had nothing to turn in, since all that we had owned was now at the bottom of the North Sea.

By now, the Germans had lists of addresses for a great number of Jewish people, which came from the Jewish Council. Orders from the Nazis now came directly to our homes via registered mail, and the Nazis saw to it that these ordinances arrived on the evenings or days of the Shabbat as well as other Jewish Holy Days, especially during Passover because they knew we would be at home. Felix visited us every night after dark. He frequently said, "I will never register in Amsterdam. Never! Never!"

One evening, our neighbor and landlord, Jan, came rushing to our room. It was June 22, 1941. He said in an excited voice, his face flushed from exertion, "Guess what . . . good news . . . I heard on the crystal [his radio] . . . can you believe it! Germany attacked Russia!" He continued with a wide grin on his face, "Boy, oh, boy, that will be the end of the master race!"

Although our worries were of a different nature, we became swept up in Jan's enthusiasm. Our excitement continued as Felix entered the room. Felix, too, was excited, but he remained more objective than the rest of us. Jan continued, "This is the beginning of the end for the Germans; you better believe it. Nobody has ever conquered Russia. I don't know whether we will survive, but I can guarantee you here and now that the Germans will lose the war." And so the conversation went on and on that night; there was a flicker of hope for all of us.

Jan's wife had also come upstairs during our animated conversation, and together we sort of celebrated the inevitable downfall—we hoped and believed—of the German Blitzkrieg and Hitler's master race. Felix, who was an expert in history, explained his view. He said, "We can't say anything for sure yet, until the winter comes. Then we will see a victory, but there will be many casualties, I'm afraid."

Suddenly, the newspapers were forbidden to write anything regarding Russian literature, Russian works of art, or anything else about Russian culture. Now the Russians were the enemies of the Germans, whereas before they were brothers and partners in war.

And so we spent many evenings together, we three families, all of us hopeful. Jan told us a lot about the resistance and how its members—on many occasions—were successful in fooling the Germans. In the beginning of the Resistance Movements, their members had little experience in this type of war situation, and many mistakes were made. Unfortunately, great numbers of these patriotic people were caught and killed.

The following is the text of an article that appeared in one of the underground newspapers, which Jan had given us. It is part of my collection of clippings from these years. The newspaper was called *De Waarheid,* meaning "The Truth."

We find ourselves in the greatest and most heinous population destruction which the world has ever seen. There is no comparison with anything else than that which the Nazi tyranny has brought upon us. We do not want fascism in the Netherlands, no anti-Semitism, no oppression, no German poison. We abhor racial hatred. CITIZENS: PROTEST.

Our fear for Jan was continuous. He told us so many secrets, such as the way the Resistance Movements made false food coupons, how they circulated all the underground newspapers, and how they knew how to set up secret connections with people in London. We emphasized to Jan and his wife to be careful, but they were young and enthusiastic for their cause and therefore saw no danger. Jan's destiny would turn out to be fatal.

One day I said to my mother, "I am quickly going to the post office to mail a letter." That special, worried look came over my mother's face as she asked me, "What letter, and to whom are you sending it?" I answered, "Well, you know, to the Schepenstraat. I want to find out where Aunt Sien and the family are."

It was against my mother's protest that I left the house. When I arrived at the post office, I did not see many people other than a German soldier standing near the entrance. I needed a stamp, so I went to the service window and asked the clerk for one. The clerk looked me over and said, "You have to first fill out a form." I must have looked quite puzzled, and I remember a feeling of claustrophobia coming over me. The clerk continued, "Are there any pictures in the letter, and did you write it in German?" He took the letter in his hands and looking me over again said, "The letter has to be open and you cannot have any crossword puzzles or chess problems or music in it." He then handed the letter back to me.

I backed up a bit and started to tear up the letter. I was about to run away when he motioned me to come to another window. Somehow I had a feeling that he was a good, patriotic citizen and that he wanted to tell me something important. He said, "Don't you know all about the new rules coming out?" His voice was almost a whisper. "The Germans want to know everything, the names and addresses of the senders, what you are writing about. You are not allowed to put the letters in the mailbox anymore. You have to show your papers." He went on and on in his low voice.

By that time, the German soldier had obviously become suspicious. He walked toward us, but I could see that he did not understand our language. I could see that he was not too bright either. The clerk ended our conversation with, "You better go home fast."

I ran out of the post office with the torn up pieces of the letter in my coat pocket. I luckily reached my home safely. I realized that, in that experience, I had gone through "the eye of a needle." There were many, many more "eyes of the needle" to come.

Chapter 15: The Last Chance

My sister, Elisabeth, had become a companion to a family with whom she lived in Amersfoort. The home was close to where my mother and I lived. Elisabeth was extremely panicky and nervous as a result of all the horrible things that were going on. Each time that we saw her she said, "If we die, we will see each other in the hereafter." Her mind had been filled with these thoughts since the time of the invasion when the Germans rang our doorbell for utensils.

In the meantime, Felix's sister, Nellie, had met a young man who also was a refugee from Germany. He and his mother, who was sickly, lived not far from us. Amersfoort, at that time, was still a small town. I divided my time as best I could among all my family and friends. I have not mentioned before that we had extended family living in Amersfoort: the van Zuidens, who were my mother's full cousins. Both brothers van Zuiden had nice stores in the center of Amersfoort. One aunt and uncle had a men's clothing store, and the other family members, my Uncle Isse and his wife, Aunt Serien, were the owners of a popular and elegant ladies apparel boutique on the Varkensmarkt.

During this terrible time all of us felt dazed and bewildered; everything we did seemed aimless. Whenever we got together, we talked about our lovely country, Holland, and how it had become a theater of hell. All of us knew that we could not expect anything good for the future with the Germans in charge, especially when we read in the newspapers how they planned to eradicate the Jewish population.

A tiny flicker of hope came one day in the winter of 1941, when Felix received a letter from the German Consul's Office indicating that we could get our exit visas to immigrate to Cuba. Shortly after the invasion, Felix had gone to the German Consulate to apply for us and several family members for exit visas. We were willing to go anywhere! For a year we had not heard a word from the Consulate's Office regarding our applications, but now, one year later, this letter reached us from the German Immigration Department. At the time, we truly believed that this was our opportunity to escape the Nazis.

The letter directed us to come to a special office in Amsterdam that was set up solely for Jewish people. The letter included a great number of instructions as to what to bring with us: passports, x-rays, family history, and a certain amount of money. Frantically, we gathered everything together for the appointed time. When all of this was done, Nellie, her boyfriend Kurt, Felix, and I set off by train to Amsterdam.

I distinctly remember what a terrible, sleepless night I had the night before we left, with nightmares and stomach upsets. Deep in my heart, I felt that no good would come of this—once again, I had that feeling of impending doom. But outwardly, I kept my calm.

When we arrived at the office in Amsterdam, we were ordered to stand on a yellow painted line. We were forbidden to speak. There were a lot of Jewish people who had gone there for the same purpose: to get a visa to exit Holland. The officials made us stand there on that yellow line for a long, long time. Upon seeing the swastikas and Nazi flags, we almost wanted to turn back. When our turn finally came, I looked at the German official sitting behind the window. Never in my life had I seen such hatred in anyone's eyes. In later years, I would often remember his face; in fact, even now, that face haunts me from time to time, and I have even had nightmares about the experience.

After questioning us extensively, the official handed us a document stating that Cuba had confirmed an entry visa for us. We had to pay a sum of money for which we received a confirmation. Finally, the four of us left Amsterdam with our documents in hand. They had kept our passports, informing us that they would be mailed to us after Berlin had confirmed our arrangements!

When we arrived home and analyzed the situation, we came to the conclusion that it would have been better had we not gone to Amsterdam at all. As it turned out, we never received our passports in the mail, nor did we hear from Cuba. The Germans had gotten richer from all of the money they had collected from the Jewish people.

We discussed our experiences with the family and with the Kolkmans, our neighbors downstairs. Jan remarked, "How could you have gone? You know that you cannot trust the Germans. All they want is your money."

There was not much information broadcast on the crystal radio about the fate of our Jewish fellowmen in other countries that were occupied by the Germans. We could only guess their future by what we were experiencing in Holland. So far, the news from the "free world" did not include any news about the treatment of the Jews.

All we heard on the Nazi-controlled radio was continuous boasting by the Germans of their victories, speeches by Seyss-Inquart that soon the war would be over, and that Hitler would accomplish a total victory with the annihilation of all Jews. But we also heard on Jan's crystal radio that at some date in 1941, the British had destroyed the large German battleship, the *Bismarck*. The Dutch press was not allowed to mention much about it in the newspapers; they were limited to only a few lines.

The year 1941 turned out to be such a bad year that at one point my mother became quite ill. Her illness was the result of a combination of nerves, stress, worry, and depression. We needed a doctor but were not allowed to seek the services of a Christian doctor, and Jewish doctors were forbidden to practice any longer. We turned to Jan for advice. He immediately contacted a physician, Dr. Haring, whom Jan described as a good, patriotic citizen. Dr. Haring came to our home in the evening hours and treated my mother on many occasions until she recuperated. I shall never forget this kind man. Later on, when the worst crimes against the Jewish people were committed, Dr. Haring was instrumental in pre-dating written exemptions for those who were ordered to concentration camps. However, the Germans simply did not take any notice of them. Of course, we did not get our passports returned to us or any extensions via the Jewish Council.

In the meantime, I often visited my aunt and uncle, Isse and Serien van Zuiden. It always gave me a lift to be with them in their elegant shop. Their

My Uncle Isse van Zuiden

living quarters were upstairs over their boutique; this was quite customary in Holland during those times. Their shop was not too far from where I lived, and I walked there and spent some days helping them out, sorting through merchandise, and returning dresses to the racks.

One day a heartbreaking tragedy took place right in the presence of my aunt and myself. We had discovered a huge swastika at the entrance of the store. My uncle, in his innocence, said, "We have to clean it up immediately." I went to get a broom from the back of the closet, and then we diligently began to try to remove it. Suddenly, an SS official stormed in from nowhere, shouting in German to both my uncle and me; then he attacked my uncle with a heavy object. My aunt and I began to scream, but we were powerless to help. Several of Hitler's SS army men dragged my uncle away—we learned he was taken to the concentration camp in Amersfoort.

The Rabbi of the Jewish community and many of our friends tried desperately to get my uncle back home. After six weeks in the concentration camp he did come home—a broken man with many serious head wounds. My aunt and family tried to nurse my poor uncle back to some physical recovery. But a short time later, the Nazis came to take him back to the camp where they immediately beat him to death.

This heinous incident had a devastating effect not only on my relatives, and especially my aunt, but also on the entire Jewish community in Amersfoort. The boutique was closed; it never opened again.

When we talked to Felix and his family the night after my uncle was killed, Felix said, "The enormity of the tragedies that the Germans will bring upon us is not fully understood by the Dutch. The Jewish Council still thinks it is doing us a favor by accommodating and cooperating with the Germans. All of us are doomed if we don't get out of here. I will fight to the last minute."

My uncle was fifty-six years old when he died. I grieved for him; I grieved for humanity. I grieved for our future. I realized that with the Germans in my country, everything we had known—culture, refinement, civility—was gone.

THE DEPORTATIONS

Chapter 16: The Razzias

The pogroms and deportations began. The "Hinnom," the hell, had become a reality for us; our world as we knew it was gone. Ghettos were created by the Nazis, first in the big cities. Entire areas were fenced in and staked out with large signs, printed with big letters that read, "JEWISH AREA ONLY." Jewish people were not allowed to leave their homes between 6:00 P.M. and 6:00 A.M. We were required to put signs on our homes that read, "Jewish locale."

My mother and I should not have been residing in a non-Jewish home. This was terribly humiliating and provoked the utmost fear within us. But the Kolkmans were not afraid of the Germans and in typical Dutch fashion told us, "Don't pay attention to the Rot-Moffen," which meant "those crazy Germans."

Although we had been aware of the systematic eradication of the Jewish population in Germany, I felt during this time that the evil forces of the German occupation were not completely understood by us innocent, and somewhat gullible, Dutch Jews. At the time, we still underestimated the evil of the Nazis. Soon, however, we realized what the Germans were capable of. They began to pick up people right from the streets of the cities; then they tortured and killed them. It seemed that their actions depended upon their moods and that they did not have to account for their evil crimes to anyone. Until the deportations began, the suicides among the Jewish people grew to epidemic proportions.

On December 7, 1941, Jan ran up the stairs to our place, his eyes almost bulging from their sockets. His face was flushed with excitement as he said,

"I just heard on my crystal that the Japanese bombed Pearl Harbor. It is a terrible disaster for the Americans. I am sure that America will now get into the war." We spent the entire evening talking about the bombing of Pearl Harbor and guessing what the next events would be. The next morning we learned that America had declared war on Japan, whereafter Germany declared war on America. The Germans and the Japanese had now become partners in evil! Again, we became swept up in Jan's enthusiasm. We were certain that the Germans would lose the war. But when? And would it be too late for the Jewish people?

The Germans became much bolder and no longer committed their crimes in secret. Right after America became embroiled in the war, Seyss-Inquart gave an abominably long speech directed at America and, once again, Jews. His speech appeared on the front pages of all of the news-papers. He claimed that America would "spend milliards and milliards," which translated means "billions and billions of dollars" but would lose the war anyway. He went so far as to accuse the Jews of causing the tragedy at Pearl Harbor and claimed that Jews ruined patriotism throughout the world. Seyss-Inquart assured his listeners that Germany would destroy American ships. He ended his speech with "Germany will win for the entire world." As young as I was at the time, I figured that such statements could only originate from the mind of an insane person, and I wondered what evil genes the Germans carried within them.

I am not sure of the exact origin of the word *razzia*, but it carried a meaning of doom. It meant "round-up," or a "raid on suspects." It certainly meant death for us. Between the hours of curfew, the razzias began. The Germans would enter certain areas where Jews resided, herd them up, throw them into trucks, and deport them to Westerbork, the dreaded processing camp in the north of Holland. It made no difference to the Germans if they were old or sick. If the elderly were bedridden, the Nazis used water hoses to make them get out of bed, or dogs who were trained to viciously bite people. Then the Nazis dragged these critically ill and injured people into the trucks.

The homes of these Jews were then sealed, and the Germans had the freedom to steal whatever they fancied. There was a foreman of the SS in Holland by the name of J. H. Feldmeyer. It was widely known that after rounding up Jewish people and deporting them, he helped himself to valuable items in their homes: art, antiques, jewelry, and even furniture, which he shipped off to Germany.

Many protest letters were addressed to Seyss-Inquart, to Rauter, and to other high officials in the German occupation. I have in my collection copies of many of these letters, especially from Catholic bishops. As a result of these protests, hundreds of Catholics were deported to Germany to "work for the war machine." Most of them never returned. Non-Jews were strictly prohibited from entering Jewish areas, which were partitioned by barbed wire.

In the meantime, everyone in Holland suffered from continuous air raids for which we were not prepared. Allied planes sometimes hit civilian areas, and innocent people were killed. Jan often told us how, on many occasions, the Resistance Movements came to the aid of the British pilots whose planes had been shot down. The underground movements became more and more experienced in eluding the Nazis. They were not afraid to act quickly in dangerous situations.

Felix still had cousins living in the outskirts of Rotterdam with whom his brother Theo had contact. These family members included a husband, wife, and two small sons. The husband had been the head of the grain company where Felix and Theo had been employed. In December of 1941, we learned from Theo that there was a possibility for his cousins—and also for Theo—to escape Holland through Switzerland. There was so much chaos and confusion at the time that the possibility of this slipped in and out of our minds but did not seem a reality at first. One did not know what to think or what the next minute would bring. But as luck—or perhaps fate—would have it, Theo and the family made it over the Dutch border early in 1942. Felix's mother prayed day and night, not knowing how to cope with the emptiness that Theo's departure had left behind.

The cousins had lived for years in a stately home, which was elegantly furnished. The home featured a collection of some of the most breathtaking paintings and art objects. Felix had told me, before his brother and this family had escaped, that he would try to save the contents of the house. I paid little attention to this; I was very distraught over the disappearance of several Jewish people I had known so well who had been taken during the night by the Nazis, never to be seen or heard from again.

But when Theo and his cousins had fled Holland, Felix arranged for the owner of a moving company in Amersfoort, a patriotic person, to help him load many of the valuables from the home into the truck. This had been a daring venture; I was upset that Felix had done this because it placed his life in great risk. If someone had noticed him, or betrayed him, it would have been the end of his life. But Felix and his friend succeeded in loading the truck with as much as they could and transporting it to Amersfoort in good condition. The valuables were hidden in a secret place in the owner's home in Amersfoort. And, of course, we were overjoyed that Felix was safe.

When I told my mother what Felix had done, she turned white. "I'm glad that you didn't tell me," she said. "But what we should do now is pack some suitcases again with all the photographs and our belongings." Her face was forlorn. "I will ask the Kolkmans if we could leave everything here." She continued, "In case something should happen to us and we have to go." Her words, "in case we have to go," have haunted me forever. There had been no hope in her voice. There was only surrender.

Chapter 17: The Star

The deportations continued and many of our family and friends disappeared. The ultimate degradation came in May of 1942.

All Jewish people were ordered to wear the Star of David. We were ordered to appear in person at an office in Amersfoort to pick up and pay for the Stars of David, which were made of a dreadful yellow cloth. In the center of each star, in big, black letters, the word "Jew" was printed. Each Star of David came with instructions on how and where to put it on one's coat, dress, or suit so that it would be visible for anyone to see. Of course the instructions also came with the usual threats in the event that one would not adhere to the rules.

In protest of this absurd situation, many Christian people also began to wear stars on their clothing. However, warnings immediately appeared in the newspapers informing the Christian population of the consequences that they would face should they continue to wear stars in protest. The Germans knew all too well how to instill fear in the hearts of people.

It seemed that the Germans felt it their right to detain anyone for any reason if he or she was wearing the Star of David. One never knew what would happen; so much depended on the temperament of the Nazi at the moment of detainment. Some Jewish people were sent away, never to be seen or heard from again.

Following this latest order, my sister came right away to the flat where we lived. She was terribly upset, and the anger in her eyes was like shooting fire. She blurted, "I will never wear that idiot star. Never! Never!" Looking at both my mother and me, my sister continued, "I am getting married to Abraham and then we'll go into hiding. All of our Christian neighbors in the street are wearing the star just to pester those damned Germans." She continued with a flood of curses directed at the Germans.

My sister was very beautiful at the time. She had big blue eyes tinged with a hint of green, lovely golden brown hair, and peach skin, which most women from the Northern countries were blessed with. She was a natural beauty. We had known for quite a while that she had become acquainted with a gentleman from the family where she had been staying. Mama and I had met him a number of times, and he struck us as a fine and intelligent man with a warm personality. He must have been at least twenty-five years older than my sister. Over the months that we knew him, he had hinted several times to my mother that he would like to marry my sister.

In those years many marriages took place that under normal circumstances might not have happened or would have been postponed. My mother and I took in all of this; we were happy for my sister inasmuch as one could think of happiness at that time. My mother said to my sister when she announced her upcoming marriage, "Will Mr. Van Dam do the wedding? Is he still here? And where will it be held?" My mother continued, "I am happy that you are getting married to a good person who will take care of you."

My sister had never been a religious person. It had always been difficult to get her to go to Synagogue, even under normal circumstances. But she said, "Abraham has contacted Mr. Van Dam; he will just marry us and then we will go into hiding." We asked her, "Where will you go?" She answered, "Oh, Abraham knows lots of farmers in Hoogland and Nijkerk. They will help us; I will leave it all up to Abraham."

Mr. Van Dam was our beloved Rabbi. He functioned in Amersfoort as Rabbi, Cantor, Hebrew teacher, and besides all of this, as an inspector of ethnic foods to insure that all were kosher, according to Jewish law.

He was known as "Mr. Van Dam" because for anything that was out of the realm of his usual work, we had to go to one of the chief Rabbis, of which there were four where I grew up in Holland. In my district the Chief Rabbi was the honorable Justus Tal.

As my sister continued her ranting and raving, my mother interrupted her by saying, "You are an adult now, but remember, if you don't wear the star and they ask you for your papers, they will take you . . . " My sister sneered, as if she was no longer afraid. She was probably strengthened by the prospect of getting married to someone who could make decisions for her. I kept my mouth shut during their conversation, but I was thinking, "With or without a star, the Nazis will do away with us in any case."

I got up from my chair and embraced my sister, wishing her well. My mother did the same. My sister then left with another stream of curses against the Germans.

We could not go to her wedding, which was just a quick formality; it was too dangerous for us to leave our house. I did not hear from my sister again until four years later, after the war. For my mother, it was the last time she embraced her daughter.

Chapter 18: The Summons

It was now mid-June 1942. Early one morning, Felix left for Amsterdam to try—in one last, frantic attempt—to get some papers from the Jewish Council for postponement of deportation for ourselves and for both of our families. Reluctantly, we said good-bye to him. We had learned from the Resistance Movements, via the Kolkmans, that the offices of the Jewish Council were a madhouse. Jan told us that thousands of Jewish people stood in line for hours trying to register for exemptions. The members of the council—honorable and deserving citizens I am sure—were suddenly faced with totally unforeseen circumstances, having trusted the Germans on false promises that the council would be in charge of its own people. But now, the council was at the mercy of monsters and beasts. There were rumors that by a certain date in the near future all Jews of Amersfoort would have to leave; Amersfoort was to become *Judenrein*, translated from the German, "Free of Jews."

Later that morning on the day that Felix left for Amsterdam, I received a dreadful announcement in the mail stating that I was required to report for work in Germany. The announcement listed the date and hour that I was to report to a train station in Hooghalen for a medical examination, which was to take place in the presence of the German police. I became almost hysterical.

The summons came from the *Zentralstelle Fur Judische Auswanderung*, meaning, "Central Office for Jewish Resettlement." The summons contained three pages. For the sake of history, I am listing most of its contents. I was required to bring the following items with me:

> one suitcase
> one pair of boots
> one pair of stockings
> two pieces of underwear

one work outfit
one sweater
two blankets
two sheets
one plate, one drinking cup, one spoon
one towel and some soap
enough food to last three days

I was also required to hand over food coupons at the station when I arrived.

Then came endless instructions on how to pack: a large suitcase was to be marked with my last name, first name, date of birth, and the word *Holland*. I was forbidden to take anything else from my home, and I was warned that pets were not allowed.

Then, with more threats came the following order: sickness was no excuse to forego this ordinance. If a person was sick on the day of departure, then a German doctor would come for inspection along with the Gestapo. The summons continued with further orders: homes had to be locked up and keys put in one's travel bag. The summons had to be shown to the train personnel. The following documents had to be packed in a separate bag:

bank accounts and bankbooks
savings accounts
stocks, bonds, and names of those who owed us money
life insurance, scholarship papers, and funeral funds with
   the location of the plots
credits from Holland or other countries
keys and numbers of safe deposit boxes
inheritances, interests from inheritances
rights of patents or real estate
art of any kind
collector's items
jewelry, diamonds, gold and/or silver objects, such as medals
any other valuables
gifts

OPROEPING!

Aan   L   No.

U moet zich voor eventueele deelname aan een, onder politietoezichtstaande, werkverruiming in Duitschland voor persoonsonderzoek en geneeskundige keuring naar het doorgangskamp Westerbork, station Hooghalen, begeven.

Daartoe moet U op _____ om _____ uur

op de verzamelplaats _____ aanwezig zijn

Als bagage mag medegenomen worden:

    1 **koffer of rugzak**
    1 **paar werklaarzen**
    2 **paar sokken**
    2 **onderbroeken**
    2 **hemden**
    1 **werkpak**
    2 **wollen dekens**
    2 **stel beddengoed (overtrek met laken)**
    1 **eetnap**
    1 **drinkbeker**
    1 **lepel en**
    1 **pullover**
    handdoek en toiletartikelen

en eveneens marschproviand voor 3 dagen en alle aan U uitgereikte distributiekaarten met inbegrip van de distributiestamkaart.

De mee te nemen bagage moet in gedeelten gepakt worden.

a.   **Noodzakelijke reisbehoeften**

daartoe behooren: 2 dekens, 1 stel beddegoed, levensmiddelen voor 3 dagen, toiletgerei, etensbord, eetbestek, drinkbeker,

b.   **Groote bagage**

De onder b. vermelde bagage moet worden gepakt in een stevige koffer of rugzak, welke op duidelijke wijze voorzien moet zijn van **naam, voornamen, geboortedatum en het woord „Holland".**

Gezinsbagage is niet toegestaan.

Het voorgaande moet nauwkeurig in acht genomen worden, daar de groote bagage in de plaats van vertrek afzonderlijk ingeladen wordt.

De verschillende bewijs- en persoonspapieren en distributiekaarten met inbegrip van de distributiestamkaart mogen **niet bij de bagage verpakt worden,** doch moeten, voor onmiddellijk vertoon gereed, medegedragen worden.

De woning moet ordelijk achtergelaten en afgesloten worden, de huissleutels moeten worden medegenomen.

Niet medegenomen mogen worden: levend huisraad.

K 372

The Summons

transfers (promises for future gifts)
compensations from insurance companies
a list of any debts
accurate descriptions of partnerships, with names, addresses,
    and telephone numbers of the partners
partnerships in land, real estate, and other business ventures
possessions or interests of any kind in provinces, cities,
    and/or any other country
mortgages
land registry numbers

At the bottom of page three of the summons in large letters, it read:

ON THE DAY OF YOUR DEPARTURE YOU WILL GET A
FREE TRAVEL PERMIT.

ANYONE NOT COMPLYING WITH THESE ORDERS
WILL BE HEAVILY PUNISHED.

The summons was signed by SS Hauptsturmfuhrer Woerlein.

The shock I felt was indescribable. My mother and I clung together in desperation. Jan and his wife came upstairs. They said to me, "Don't go! We all know what this is all about. They cannot keep track of everything and everyone."

I could not picture myself in a German camp working for the German war efforts. I took the summons and put it in the bag with my other papers that I had carefully kept hidden. Somehow I pretended that I had never seen the summons, which was, of course, hiding my head like an ostrich. I did not want my mother to know how deeply upset I was.

After the Kolkmans had left, I said to my mother, "There is hardly anything to eat in the house. I have to go to the store and buy some food." My mother became alarmed and, embracing me, pleaded, "Please don't go! With that star, they might pick you up." For a long while, we remained in our mother-daughter embrace. In silence, our thoughts were like windmills in a vicious storm.

THE HIDING YEARS

Chapter 19: The Encounter

I don't know how I got the strength, but I just pretended, for my mother's sake, that I had never seen the summons.

We did need something to eat and I was adamant to get food. There were still some stores open to Jewish people, but by orders from the Germans, Jews could only shop on certain days of the week between the hours of three o'clock and five o'clock in the afternoon.

I waited until three o'clock; my heart was heavy with anxiety. The brilliant landscape of Holland, which I had so enjoyed in the past, with its cheerful homes, stately trees, picturesque bridges over elegant canals, and colorful flowers in full bloom now looked terrifying to me. I saw everything with different eyes. Had it been nothing more than an optical illusion in the past? My heart was heavy, and fear was my constant companion during those years. Now I wondered if Felix would come back from Amsterdam and what would happen to his family.

I reached the store safely and bought what we needed. As I was leaving, that same strange and foreboding feeling overwhelmed me again. At first I hesitated to leave, but I had to go. I stood there for a while, thinking of the summons now hidden in my closet. I felt bewildered and forlorn.

Suddenly, a tall man on his bicycle spotted me. He stopped, stepped off his bike, and approached me. He said, "What the hell are you doing here with that damned star on your blouse? Take that damned thing off and follow me." I had never seen this man before. He was very tall, a real sturdy Dutchman, fearless it seemed. For some reason I felt safe in his company; I instinctively knew I was in good hands.

I tore the star off my clothing and followed him. It was quite a long walk to his home. When we finally arrived, he motioned to me that I should go through the alley and wait for him while he parked his bike. After a few minutes he guided me through the backyard and into his home. He said, "I am Piet (pronounced Pete) Brandsen, and you are Jewish. Well, let's hear your story. What is your name? Where do you live?" As I began to talk, he interrupted and said, "Wait, let me call Dina." He removed the pipe he was smoking from his mouth and yelled, "Dina!"

Dina was his wife. I noticed immediately by the way she looked up at him that she adored him. She then looked at me and said hello. Piet said to Dina, "Get the girls here right away. I have an important matter to discuss." I heard Dina shout something out into the street, and shortly thereafter four girls came in. They all looked alike to me; all of them had white-blond hair and blue eyes.

Piet said to me, "These are our four girls. They are Beppie, who is five years old; Willie, who is seven; Henny, eleven years old; and our oldest, Nel, who is twelve." In a very serious tone he commanded all of us: "Come upstairs, where we can talk. This is a serious matter." I could tell that all four children looked up to their father with deep respect. No matter that I had just met Piet. I knew right away that he was a man of few words. The tone of his voice and his entire demeanor were so effective that he had no need to repeat anything he said. We all went to one of the upstairs bedrooms.

He turned to his family and began. "Listen carefully. This is a Jewish girl, and we all know what will happen to the Jewish people with those damned Germans around." Upon hearing this, Dina made a sign of the cross and so did the two older girls. Piet continued, "It is our duty to help. We must take her in and hide her." It sounded as simple as that! He then turned to me and said, "We want to hear your story. Tell us what is going on."

At first I was overwhelmed and speechless. Since there had not been much to eat lately, I became somewhat shaky and dizzy. My emotions, of course, contributed to my physical state. Piet pulled up some chairs. Dina and the four girls were sitting on the bed. And then I spoke freely. I told them that my mother and I lived with the Kolkman family in the Rubensstraat, that I had received the dreadful summons that morning, that I had a boyfriend who had gone to Amsterdam to try to get some extension papers. I explained that Felix and his family also lived in the Rubensstraat, that I did not know where my brother Ben or my sister were, or whether my oldest brother and his wife had gone into hiding. The words gushed out like a waterfall.

They all listened attentively. The whole time Piet smoked his pipe and appeared in deep thought. When I finished talking, he said, "I have heard of the Kolkmans; they are patriotic citizens." He then stood up and said, "I will take you home, but I will come back to your house tomorrow morning to speak with your mother and the other family." Turning to Dina and his daughters, in a stern voice he admonished them, "You are not to talk to anyone about this. If things leak out, all of us will be shot."

On our way home I told him about the shipwreck and how we had spent so many months in the hospital in England. He said to me, "You would have been smart to stay there."

When we were close to my home, I pointed out the house where Felix and his family lived. In a reassuring tone he said to me, "I will be there first thing in the morning. Bring everyone together and we shall decide how to handle all of this." I thanked him profusely and as we shook hands, he said to me, "Some day we'll get rid of those damned Rot-Moffen!"

I rushed upstairs and noted with much gratitude in my heart that Felix had returned. He looked completely worn out. I could see that he was also in a state of depression. He gave us a short account of what had happened in Amsterdam. The people at the Jewish Council had been feverishly typing out requests and medical petitions for the sick and the old. Hundreds of people had stood in line for hours. Nurses from mental institutions had literally begged the Germans to allow ill patients, who could not work anyway, to stay in Holland.

The council staff had handed out blankets, warm coats, shoes, towels, bed linens, and other items for those who were destined for the camps.

Piet Brandsen

There were people who were old, young, and sick—in every physical condition. Felix met two young people who told him about their poor diabetic father whose leg had been amputated. During a razzia, the Nazis had dragged him out of bed and thrown him into a truck that was headed for one of the camps.

When the Germans came and began to gather people up with the indisputable intention of herding them off to concentration camps, Felix fled. It had become too dangerous to stay any longer.

It was common knowledge that the large opera house in Amsterdam (De Stadsschouwburg) was the central point where Germans gathered Jewish people to deport them first to Westerbork, and from there, to Poland.

It was ghastly to listen to these things and try to absorb it all. Over and over I asked myself, as many others did, "What are the Germans made of?"

After Felix had calmed down, I told him about my encounter with Piet Brandsen. After explaining everything, I told Felix that Piet would meet with all of us the next morning. Although we were in a deep state of despair and our moods were quite grave, for the moment we believed that not all was lost. Renewing our hopes, we looked forward to our meeting with Piet the next day.

Chapter 20: Getting Married

Piet showed up the next morning, as promised. All of us met in Felix's home: Felix and his mother, Nellie and her boyfriend Kurt, and my mother and I were present. Piet radiated confidence, and I could tell that Felix and his family admired him. Our conversation focused on the German invaders, the eradication of the Jews wherever there was an occupation of Nazis, and our ideas on how long the war would last.

Piet told us that he was a contractor and involved in the Resistance Movement. He and his wife, both Catholics, believed it was their duty to help their fellow countrymen. He further explained that he had two rooms in the attic of his house; one was occupied by Dina's father, who was old and a bit senile. The other was available for us to hide in. Then, after puffing on his pipe for a few long moments, he began to speak to us in a very serious tone of voice. He said, "I know that these are extraordinary times where quick action is required." Then, looking directly at Felix and me, he continued, "We are Catholics, and in our religion it is not right to have an unmarried couple in one room." There was silence for a few minutes. Then he said, "I would advise you to get married as soon as possible, and Dina and I will be happy to have you in our home. You don't have to worry about Dina's father. I will make up a story about who you are, in the event that the neighbors ask him."

Once again, I was faced with a spur-of-the-moment decision, just like the one I made on the SS *Simon Bolivar*. Piet appeared quite calm in the midst of all of this even though this was a life-and-death matter. I knew that Felix loved me deeply. We had gone through so much together that it seemed the most natural thing in the world for us to get married before we went into hiding.

The first one to break the silence of the moment was Felix's mother, who was extremely Orthodox. She said in halting Dutch, "The Rabbi, is he still here?" We looked at one another as she continued. "One has to be married by a Rabbi in the Synagogue." Piet pointed out that this was not a time to think things over extensively or to make detailed plans. He said, "I know that Mr. Van Dam is the local Jewish spiritual leader. Let me find out what he can do and I will come back later."

My mother was an easygoing person, and under these circumstances she understood that some religious customs had to be put aside. Felix's mother, however, attached much importance to the ways of her religion.

Piet left and promised to return soon. It seemed now that Felix and I were destined to be married. Felix, turning to his sister and her boyfriend Kurt, said, "Perhaps Piet can help you also. If you have a chance to hide, don't let it slip away." But Kurt was hesitant; he still entertained illusions of escaping to Switzerland.

I suddenly began to feel very guilty. What about our mothers? Kurt also lived with his mother, who was sickly and a diabetic. What a terrible dilemma we found ourselves in! Felix's mother began to cry. She said in German, "How can I stay behind alone?" My mother said, "As long as I know that you and Felix are safe, I don't want you to worry about me." Our emotions were almost unbearable.

After a long two hours, Piet returned. He regretfully reported that he had been unable to locate Mr. Van Dam. Before the invasion, there had been four Chief Rabbis in Holland, one for each of four districts that consisted of certain provinces. Each Rabbi—learned scholars and renowned people—functioned as judge, whether it be in religious matters or in special situations. In the district of Amersfoort, in the province of Utrecht, a certain Honorable Justus Tal, a well-known scholar, had been serving the Jewish communities for many years. His home was in Utrecht, a good-sized city located about twenty kilometers northwest of Amersfoort.

And so our conversation turned to Rabbi Tal. In the course of our discussion, Piet stood up and said, "Listen, instead of spending valuable time trying to find out where Mr. Van Dam is, I will go and see if I can find Rabbi Tal, if he is still there. I will explain the situation to him."

We were embarrassed to have Piet do all of this for us, and we objected. But Piet had made up his mind and was resolved to save people. Turning to Felix and me he said, "Give me the address of Rabbi Tal. I'll go to Utrecht and tell him what is going on." Upon leaving, he turned to all of us and in a determined tone he said, "Trust me, this is just as important for me as it is for you. We have to keep fighting against the Rot-Moffen."

When he was gone, our tension began to rise. Where would all of this lead to? What does one do in hiding? How long would we have to hide? What about our mothers, our families, our friends? Would we have enough food?

Early the next morning Piet returned. We all gathered again in Felix's home. There was Piet, pipe and all, our "last-chance" friend and hero. He told us that he had found Rabbi Tal at home—in his underwear. Rabbi Tal explained that the German "gentlemen" had robbed him of practically everything: his books, religious items, his robes, and his clothes. And Rabbi Tal still called the Nazis, "gentlemen!"

The poor Rabbi had listened carefully to Piet and then said, "By all means, the young couple must be saved." Understanding that there was not much time to waste and aware of the danger for Piet to carry Hebrew papers back to Amersfoort, the Rabbi said, "I will teach you seven Hebrew words, and I give you the authority—with my blessing—to be the one to officiate at the marriage of this couple. In the eyes of God they will be considered man and wife."

But things turned out differently. Piet advised us to think things through during the night and told us he would return the next morning. Our new friend Piet was blessed with nerves of steel and a wonderful sense of humor, mixed with a dose of strong language. When he spoke, we were momentarily able to rid ourselves of the horrid thoughts in our heads. Piet had become our rock and our benefactor.

The next day we saw Piet again. The look on his face told us that everything would work out for us. For a few moments after he arrived, he smoked heavily and looked around. Then he turned to us and said, "I have bad news and I have good news." We kept our eyes on his face, anxious to

Jacob Van Dam, who married us

hear his next words. "I have thought over our situation and I honestly believe that I, as a Catholic, am not qualified to marry you. Besides, the Hebrew words are all upside down in my head; I would marry you the wrong way. But," and now his face lit up, "the good news is that I tried again, and I did locate Mr. Van Dam. I talked to him and he is willing to perform your wedding."

Felix's mother asked, "The Synagogue—is it still open?" Piet answered, "Nothing has happened there yet. I have to go home now, but I'll be back as soon as I can."

It was already the first week of July; time was running out for us. There was a deadline set by the Germans for Jewish people to leave the homes of Christians and to be deported. This deadline was now looming large! Mr. Van Dam had been my Hebrew teacher, and he had told Piet, "For Flory, I will do the wedding, provided we will all be here yet."

When Piet came back later that day, he stressed that we had to act quickly. He had heard, via the resistance, that the Germans were making their final plans for the Jews.

There were certain laws in Holland regarding marriage. First, the couple had to take out a marriage license in the city hall and fill out the papers in the registrar's office. Next, documents of intention would be placed on the outside of the city hall building for fourteen days so people had time to inspect the paperwork. So technically, a Dutch couple had to wait at least two weeks before an official wedding could take place. In addition to this, I had another obstacle. I was under age and needed my mother's approval to marry, which meant that she too would be put into danger by coming along with us to city hall.

Piet calmed us down. He said, "You must set the date. I will then talk to the clerk at city hall. I know him well; he is a good, patriotic man. I will fix it so you won't have to wait fourteen days. In fact, I will fix everything. I promise that you will be able to go from city hall directly to the Synagogue. I will confirm everything with Mr. Van Dam."

When we saw Piet the next day, he looked very content with all of the plans. He assured us that all had been arranged with Mr. Van Dam as well as with Mr. de Groot, the city clerk. I told Piet that I was still concerned about a number of things, but he did not want to hear any of it! He said jokingly, "If there are no bombs falling on our heads, everything will be all right." Then he added, "Well, if we are bombed, at least we will have our names in the newspapers!"

The date for our wedding was set for Thursday, July 9, 1942. I had always considered myself to be a romantic and an artistic person and so, despite the strange circumstances of our pending wedding day, I still wanted to wear something white. I found an old white dress on which I sewed some artificial flowers, which I took from a vase in the living room. I also found some old curtains, which in my mind, I figured would serve well as a veil. Well, the old curtains had to work—there was no time to find anything fancier! When I had completed my "creation," I tried everything on to see what I looked like. It was pathetic! But with the help of those I loved, I still had good hopes for our future.

On the day of our wedding I had to wear my everyday clothes. I took a small suitcase in which I packed my improvised wedding dress along with my make-believe veil, and off we went. Felix had brought me a bouquet of lovely flowers but for fear that it would draw too much attention from the Germans, I packed them in my suitcase as well.

Piet led the way to city hall, riding slowly on his bicycle ahead of us. Felix and I walked casually along the streets—our yellow stars prominently affixed to our clothing—as calmly as we could. Our mothers followed behind us, also wearing their stars. Thank goodness there were no air raids that day. After quite a long walk we made it safely to city hall without being halted by a Nazi. The clerk, Mr. de Groot, was waiting for us. He was a wonderful man and saw to it that our registration went quickly and smoothly. He had all of the necessary documents ready. My mother signed the papers, and Felix's mother acted as a witness. We then received our family register booklet—without the royal seal and without our Dutch motto, Je Maintiendrai.

These first steps went well. We now had to head for the Synagogue, which was quite a distance away. Again, Piet rode his bike ahead of us.

Although damaged, I treasure this photo of Felix and me on our wedding day

On the way to the Synagogue we heard airplanes, but somehow we made it safely.

When we arrived at the Temple, I was anxious to get out of my dress with the yellow star. I immediately went to the annex school building where I had spent many happy hours in my youth. I quickly changed my drab, everyday dress and put on my "wedding" dress. Felix put on a dark suit and a tie, and together we walked into the Synagogue, where some friends and intermarried family members were waiting for us. My brother Ies and his wife, who were not yet in hiding, arrived a bit later.

Mr. Van Dam, such a fine man, performed our wedding ceremony in a most dignified way, despite the crazy and unusual circumstances. He made the ceremony so beautiful that to this day his sermon is engraved in my heart. He began with a verse from the Book of Ecclesiastes, as spoken by Koheleth, son of King David:

> Utter futility! All is futile!
>
> One generation goes, another comes, but the earth remains
> the same forever. There is a season for everything:
> A time for being born, and a time for dying
> A time for weeping and a time for laughing
> A time for reaping and a time for sowing.

Mr. Van Dam continued his beautiful oration, applying the sermon to the circumstances of our time. His conclusion touched me deeply. He pointed out that according to Jewish custom, upon the completion of any of the five books of the Torah, the entire congregation must recite the words, "Be strong, be strong, and let us strengthen one another." (In Aramaic, the words are *Chazak, chazak ve ' nischazak*). Mr. Van Dam then explained that we were going through similar tribulations as those in the times the scriptures were written. He said when a person goes from one heartbreak to another, these words must be recited. And especially in a marriage, the words are recited twice so that one will give strength to the other.

Mr. Van Dam handed us the marriage certificate made out in Hebrew. After a warm embrace for me and a handshake for Felix, the ceremony was over. We were to be the last couple to be married in that lovely, two-hundred-year-old Synagogue. Shortly after our wedding, Mr. and Mrs. Van Dam were deported to a concentration camp, never to return again. The Synagogue was broken down by the Germans and used as a storage building during the war.

We had to return home. I quickly changed back into my old clothing and affixed the yellow star. We then began the long walk home accompanied by our family and friends. Nellie, Felix's sister, had graciously prepared some refreshments for us. The short, precious time we had together came quickly to an end.

The greatest gift and wonderful surprise on our wedding day was the arrival of my favorite cousin, Jacob de Haas of Rotterdam. He arrived without the yellow star on his clothes and without having mentioned to his parents that he was going to visit us in honor of our wedding. He took a terrible risk, and I shall never forget it. Jews still traveling by train or bus were required to show their papers to the conductor. As I mentioned before, we never realized the serious risks we took each moment! Thank goodness my cousin returned home safely. We were grateful to find out about his safety from friends of ours in the Resistance Movement.

Piet had assured our families that he would immediately try to find hiding places for everyone. Felix and I, now husband and wife, hastily packed up some of the most necessary items to take with us to our hiding place. I had finally told my mother about the secret newspaper clippings I had collected and where I had hidden

My cousin Jacob de Haas

them. She told me that she had already given the Kolkmans a number of suitcases to keep for us, "just in case . . . "

We said a tearful good-bye to our mothers and other family members, convinced that they too would find safe hiding places. I embraced my mother over and over. She seemed at peace knowing that we were in good hands with Piet.

At nightfall of this memorable day, we walked to our "honeymoon suite," a room in the attic of Piet's house, beginning another chapter of our journey through the "Valley of Death."

Chapter 21: The Hiding Place

We safely reached the home of Piet who, as always, had walked ahead of us all of the way. I remember that on this day it was raining, and when we set off, darkness had set in. Not many people were out on the streets.

Piet and Dina's house was a typical Dutch home: on the street-level was the sitting room, looking out to the backyard. This room had a small annex, which in Dutch was called the "serre." In reality, this room served no purpose. But the front room—the best room—was reserved only for visitors or for Sunday morning special occasions. Upstairs were several bedrooms and above those, on the next level, was the attic. This attic had two small rooms, one of which was Opa's. There was only one toilet for the family, and unfortunately, it was located way back in the yard, which as it would turn out, was a great handicap. There was a large kitchen parallel to the sitting room. The kitchen door was open all of the time.

Dina received us warmly. She said, "Make yourself at home while I get the tea." All four children were staring at us as they sat around the large table in the center of the kitchen. I believe that both Felix and I were very tense when we first arrived, but the warmth and the kindness of this family soon made us feel more at ease.

Piet confided completely in his wife and their four children because he began to speak freely about the resistance, how he would build hiding places, and ways that he would invent secret signs and codes in case strangers would come to visit.

This night, Piet turned to Dina and exclaimed, "Dina, you must act casually. Do not change anything in your daily habits. I do not want the neighbors to become suspicious." To the children he admonished, "Just go ahead and play with your friends. Do everything that you always do, but do not utter a word to anyone about these two people who from now on will live with us." His stern look kept everyone in silence.

The children were to call us Uncle Jan and Aunt Marie; it turned out that they had family in Belgium by these names. Piet said to them, "Should anyone ever become suspicious or come to find something out, then these two people are your real aunt and uncle from Belgium." Soon the four girls were sent to bed. They were adorable and in time I became quite fond of them. After the girls were asleep, Piet continued his conversation with us. He said in a reassuring and determined voice, "The first thing we must do is get you entirely new identity papers. I will contact my people in the resistance and explain everything." We nodded agreeably. We just sat there, not knowing what to expect in the home of total strangers.

Felix then said, "Is there possibly any chance at all to escape over the border to Switzerland?" Piet stopped smoking for a moment. He said, "Let me talk to someone whom I know well and I will see what I can do." It had become quite late and Dina, getting up from the table, said, "Let's go upstairs. We all need a good night's sleep." Then turning to us with a smile she continued, "We'll show you to your room."

Three of four Brandsen girls: Nel, Henny, and Willie; Bep, the youngest, is missing from this photograph

A great surprise awaited us. Rather than having us stay in the attic, they insisted that we use their own spacious bedroom. Felix protested. "How can we accept this?" he said. "It is too much." But Piet explained, "Look here. In the attic you have to deal with Opa. In this room there is a balcony, so at least you can get some fresh air now and then." I'm sure he said this to make us feel better about using their room. We thanked them profusely, and as they left Dina gave me a big hug and said, "Pretty soon we will get rid of the Rot-Moffen."

In the Dutch language before the war, the word *mof* was used as a nickname for a German national. As I understood it, the word *mof* dated back to World War I when the German soldiers had to wear handmuffs when they were fighting the Russians in the horrendously cold winters. *Muff* translated into Dutch is *mof*. But now, during the terrible time of the German invasion, the word *mof* had the connotation of a curse word. The Dutch people added the word *rot* to it, and so it became *rot-mof*.

Piet and Dina had warned us not to pay attention to Opa, the old man. They had told him that we were family members from far away in Belgium. In time, Opa referred to us as "the damned Belzen" because all too often, he had to use the W.C. (water closet) back in the yard when one of us was using it. If we heard Dina talking to the neighbors, we knew we could not be seen going up to our room so we had to hold on firmly to a feeble lock in the door while Opa was on the other side cursing us, trying to get in. Those were very tense moments.

Opa was in a very advanced stage of senility; none of the family members could carry on a conversation with him. I saw the girls occasionally going to his room to bring food. Sometimes he ate something while he was in the kitchen. Dina always had a large pot of soup or some other food on the stove and so Opa could help himself whenever he was hungry or felt like eating. As time went by, Opa thought of an easier way to relieve himself. He used the chamber pot, then threw the pot with all its contents out of his attic room window. The pot—and the contents—always landed on our balcony!

I had noticed a good number of religious figures in the house. Above our bed hung a large crucifix with the Christ figure attached to it. On a table in the corner of the bedroom stood a Madonna with Child. Everything was so overwhelming for me that I cried most of the time, which was not a good thing for a new bride. I kept thinking of my mother and of Felix's family, but I would not dare burden Piet at that time with my deep sorrow.

The four girls were marvelous. I instinctively knew that we could trust them not to speak to anyone about us. Their parents had given them an excellent moral upbringing. We liked the girls from the beginning of our stay, and during those first two weeks we felt that they were fond of us, too, especially Henny, the ten year old, who clung to me on every occasion that we saw each other.

To this day, I am still in awe of the children's reaction to their "new" aunt and uncle who had come to stay in their home. They never asked a thing, and there was never a hint on their part about the horrors that took place on the streets around them. They seemed to automatically understand the strong admonitions from their parents to not say a word to anyone about Felix and me. The girls were still on summer vacation from school and went about their typical days, spending lots of time with us upstairs in addition to doing chores and playing with friends. They really liked "Uncle Jan" and "Aunt Marie." For them it was a welcome change from the regular routine in their home. In the meantime, the war escalated and so did the horrors that the Germans inflicted on so many innocent people.

I missed my mother terribly, but Piet was constantly in touch with both of our families. He did, however, have to be very careful not to be seen too often in the Rubensstraat. Of course, Felix and I exchanged messages with our families via Piet, but these messages were never written. We could not put him in danger; we feared that a German would search him and find our notes.

Felix and I talked endlessly about escaping to Switzerland, wondering, on the one hand, if we could leave our mothers, and on the other hand, the dangers we would bring upon the Brandsen family if we stayed. It was tortuous to decide what to do. I kept thinking, "Would there ever be an end to all of this chaos? And where might my brother Ies and his wife be? What about my sister and her husband? Where was my brother Ben?"

We wanted to do something for Piet and his family, but it seemed as if nothing could possibly reciprocate his bravery. Nonetheless, we told them we'd do anything at all: help with housework, help the children with their schoolwork, sew, mend, whatever. It turned out—as strange as it seems now—that the most important issue in the household was that the two youngest girls needed help with their catechism lessons. I was only too happy to oblige.

Meanwhile, Dina adhered to her husband's admonition that she continue her usual routines, including talking with her neighbors at the front door of their home. These neighborly conversations sometimes lasted for an hour or more, and during that time there was no way for either of us to use the bathroom.

After a few weeks, Piet told us that we would finally get to meet "Moltjeveer," his friend from the Resistance Movement. He was to bring us new identity papers and discuss hiding places for my mother, Felix's family, and Kurt. We would also discuss with him the possibility of escaping over the border to Switzerland.

That night after the children had gone to bed, the four of us sat around the kitchen table. A special knock on the door let Piet know that someone from the Resistance Movement was outside; it was "Moltjeveer." "Moltjeveer" was his pseudonym; he was a very important leader in the Resistance Movement at the time and could not risk using his real name. He was a short, skinny man, about fifty years of age. His hair was grayish-blond and he wore glasses. When he spoke, it was evident that this man was intelligent and dedicated to his cause.

He handed us our new identity papers. We were fascinated with how authentic they looked. My photograph even captured the scar on my neck, a remnant of the tragedy of the SS *Simon Bolivar*. "Moltjeveer" said to us, "You must get to know your new names and all of the details contained in these papers." Felix was now "Jan Van Ophuizen," and I was now "Hendrika Helmina Geijtenbeek." The papers also included false birth dates and addresses and were stamped properly, including the words "valid for five years." The papers also read "MISUSE IS PUNISHABLE!"

It was amazing to us what the Resistance Movement could accomplish. We thanked both "Moltjeveer" and Piet profusely, realizing what danger the acts placed them in. Our conversation then turned to hiding places for our families and the possibility of crossing the border. "Moltjeveer" said to us, "There definitely is a possibility that people could be smuggled from Belgium to France, then escape into Switzerland. But it is a dangerous undertaking. If you want to take the risk, you must make up your mind quickly and let me know tomorrow night. I will contact our most reliable people. I'll return here tomorrow night at the same time." Felix looked at me, and I at him. Then the four of us talked until quite late.

Back in our room, Felix and I weighed the pros and cons of escaping. Felix said to me, "I have a feeling the war will last much longer than we originally thought. How can we impose on these brave people? It might take years." It was one of the most awful decisions of our lives. I agreed that we did not want to jeopardize their lives and the lives of their children. Food was becoming scarce, and there was the possibility that someone might betray us and turn us in to the Nazis. Our thoughts were wild and confused—as if we were in a vortex!

Finally, we decided to leave, and early the next morning we told Piet we decided to attempt to cross the border. Although we saw a look of shock on

False identification papers

his face, his voice remained calm, and he said he would contact "Moltjeveer." With his hand on the doorknob as he left our room, he turned to us and said, "As far as Dina and I are concerned, you can stay here with us as long as the war is on." We were deeply touched but resolved in our decision.

Later that day, Piet came back to our room and said to us, "I told 'Moltjeveer' of your decision; it is now in the hands of the Resistance Movement. Since time is of the essence, you must be ready to leave in a few days. Pack up only the most necessary items; be sure you have your new identity papers." Felix and I looked at each other, our hearts pounding. I remember that I could not eat a thing that day, nor could I sleep that night. How would our imminent trip turn out? Would we go by car, or would we have to cross mountains on foot? What if the Nazis did not believe who our new identity papers said we were? The questions went on and on, endlessly, in my head.

Finally the evening of our dangerous escape arrived. Someone from the Resistance Movement was to come for us and take us to a certain place, where again, others in the movement would guide us over the Dutch border. We were not told anything further than this; we were not to know or question anything more. The children had not been told about our leaving. Dina had made tea and was serving it in the front room, where the four us were sitting in large chairs waiting for the knock on the door that would signal the beginning of what would certainly be a perilous journey. Piet, as always, was smoking and appeared to be in deep concentration. Not a word was spoken, until at last Felix and I broke the silence by thanking them again for all they had done for us. I said, "Give the girls a big hug for us." Piet nodded; Dina's hand shook, the teacup rattling.

It was one of those evenings, similar to many in the past, where my emotions—anxiety, tension, foreboding—were magnified. I felt my heart beating fast, but I kept up my outwardly calm demeanor. Felix held tight to a small travelbag in which he had packed some toilet articles and shaving supplies. Whatever money we had was also in the bag.

In the corner of the room was a large grandfather's clock, which would peal a loud clang every fifteen minutes. Paintings and religious figures in the room shook back and forth each time the clock let out its horrendous clang. It was one of those warm summer evenings with no breeze. The clock tracking every moment, the ominous silence, the stillness in the air created an atmosphere of eeriness that I can still feel. I vividly remember the far-off sound of people talking in the street, a dog barking, and watching Dina mend some of the children's clothes. The waiting became almost unbearable, so much so that the loud clang of the clock seemed to pierce my eardrums every minute rather than every fifteen minutes. At ten o'clock that night, just to break the silence, I said to Piet, "Isn't it becoming too late to go over the border?" He removed the pipe from his mouth and simply shook his head.

Finally, at about eleven thirty, the special knock was heard. Piet answered the door, and there stood "Moltjeveer," his face drawn and pale. We immediately knew there was something wrong. "Moltjeveer" sat down and told us the awful news: a carefully planned transport of seven Jewish people over the border had been discovered by the Nazis, and all seven of them were shot. This tragedy left us in a state of shock; for more than an hour no one could utter a word. At some point during that hour "Moltjeveer" left; we were so devastated we did not even see him leave. Finally, Felix and I went upstairs to our room. Over and over in my mind I repeated the words of Mr. Van Dam, "Strength, strength, please God give us strength."

THE LABYRINTH

Chapter 22: Farewell My Loved Ones

Luckily, Piet and Dina had not said anything about our planned departure to the children. The next morning began the same as it had two weeks before, with every minute on our guard, desperately trying not to be seen or heard.

Since it was too dangerous to eat our meals downstairs where neighbors might see us, the girls always brought something to our room for us to eat. Later in the evenings we could go downstairs because the kitchen was then locked and the curtains drawn. During these evenings, Felix mostly talked to Piet about the war, the Germans, the Jewish people, and the hiding places for my mother and for Felix's family. I helped Dina in the kitchen, and afterwards, when the four girls went to bed, we made tea. It all sounds like a peaceful existence, but our minds were full of anguish. If we could only know for sure that our families would be hidden somewhere, our situation would perhaps be easier for us to bear.

"Moltjeveer" and Piet were desperately trying to find sympathetic people who were willing to take the risk of hiding Jews. We heard through Piet that a great number of Jewish couples, as well as small children and babies, had been picked up by the Nazis. Their homes had been sealed, and they were sent to Camp Westerbork from where they were immediately transported.

Through Piet, we were still in touch with my mother and Felix's family. I yearned to see my mother, but it could not be. Piet told us that my brother's store had been sealed up, and Piet was not able to find his whereabouts. It was simply too dangerous for Piet to be seen so much in town attempting to find out information.

During this time Felix started keeping a diary, which, of course, he hid upstairs very carefully. Piet also had a crystal (radio) so well hidden that even a clever German would not be able to find it. We knew from the BBC how the war was progressing, where the English armies were, what the Americans did, about the meetings between Churchill and Roosevelt, and especially how the Russians courageously fought against the Germans.

The Germans had now established several more detention camps in Holland. I remember that there was one in Vught (a small city in the province of NoordBrabant, in the south); another one in Putten, to the north, and of course the one in Amersfoort where my Uncle Isse van Zuiden had been killed. The camp in Amersfoort turned out to be one of the most vicious. Through the resistance, we heard that the Germans were slaughtering people on a daily basis there.

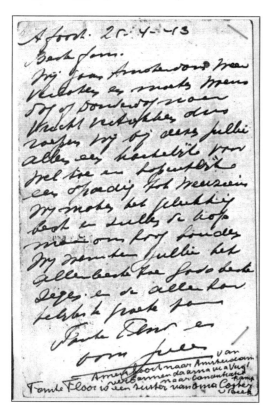

The note my uncle threw from the train

It was now eight months since January 1942, the month when the Germans announced that Holland would soon be *Judenrein,* free of Jews. There were already a great number of cities where they had taken away all Jews: Zaandam, Arnhem, Hilversum. The next target would be Amersfoort. We were all in great despair. The Germans now had the addresses of all Dutch Jews. At night they came to town, and by the next morning many Jews had been deported, forced to leave all of their belongings behind.

We learned through Piet that my beloved Aunt Flora and Uncle Jules Frank, who had so graciously received Felix's family, were still in their home in Joannes van Dieststraat. Years after the war, a diary was discovered in which my uncle recorded all of the horrible events that took place on a daily basis, up until the time that he and my aunt were deported on April 15, 1943. Many years later, I received a copy of this diary, along with a postcard dated May 10, 1943, that my uncle had thrown out of a train. On the postcard was written, "Will the finder of this card please mail this to Th. Kley, Schimmelpenninckstraat in Amersfoort." Indeed, someone had found it and mailed it. It must have been lost for many years before it was sent to us.

The deadline for the deportations neared. On Sunday, August 16, 1942 (the Hebrew month of *Ellul* 3, 5702), an order appeared in all newspapers by the German authorities commanding that all Jews between the ages of sixteen and forty be deported to Germany, and on Friday night, August 21, everyone over the age of forty would be picked up by the German police. Everyone was "allowed" to take his or her valuables, carefully packed according to Nazi-style instructions.

The Nazis also applied their rules to Jews who had converted to another religion and even to people who were mentally disabled. Seven-hundred Roman Catholics from Jewish descent also had been taken away. This was a method of revenge by the Germans, the result of a telegram sent to Seyss-Inquart by the Catholic churches in protest of the deportation of Jews.

We later learned from the resistance that among several Carmelite nuns in a convent in Limburg, in the south of Holland, was a woman named Edith Stein, born of Orthodox Jewish parents. Edith converted to Catholicism and during the war she was dragged to Camp Westerbork and then deported to Auschwitz. When the public tried to help her, she was quoted as saying, "Please don't bother for me; others need help more than I do." Edith Stein was canonized by the Catholic Church in 1998.

Around this same time telegrams were sent to all police stations stating that every day from midnight until two o'clock in the morning extra trains would be running to transport Jews to Germany, and from there to the death camps.

My mother still lived with the Kolkmans in the Rubensstraat. I had become so anxious that I could not eat or sleep. Adding to this stress was the fact that I did not want to show how anxious I was, not even to Felix. I did not want to become a burden to anyone. I was quite thin when I got married; by this time I looked emaciated. Piet, noticing how thin I had become, said, "Please don't feel shy; we have enough to eat and you must eat to keep healthy and strong." But the possible fate of my mother and other loved ones was constantly on my mind and eroded whatever strength I had.

One day, toward the end of August, "Moltjeveer" came to Piet's house and told us that he had found a hiding place for my mother. He gave the address to Piet, who would go to pick up my mother that night. I was elated, my heart pounding so hard that I thought someone would hear it beating. The evening came and with great anxiety we waited for Piet to return with good news about my mother. But when he finally arrived, we

Edith Stein

could immediately see that something was very wrong. He removed the pipe from his mouth and said, "Let's sit down. I have bad news." Turning to me he continued, "Your mother is away. I have inquired and learned that those filthy Nazis put many people on the train to Westerbork, including your mother."

Although I heard his voice explaining more, everything became a blur to me. I was incapable of hearing or understanding another word. My mother, the love of my life, in the hands of the Nazis. What would they do to her? What was her fate? Could I go on living not knowing where or how she was now? My angel mother, who would not even kill a fly. So attentive, modest, shy, soft-spoken, kind and loving; my mother in the hands of those barbarians. It was inconceivable to me.

Piet was talking, but his voice sounded distant, obscured. I vaguely heard him say something about obtaining a medical testimonial from a local doctor stating that my mother was sick and under a physician's care and not fit to travel on a transport. What had happened, I heard Piet say, was that the remainder of the Jewish community in Amersfoort had planned a last prayer meeting in the Synagogue to bid farewell to their beloved country and to commemorate the upcoming festival of the Jewish New Year, Rosh Hashanah, which, that year fell on the first days of September. My mother had left her home to attend but was picked up by the Germans. Several weeks later, we received a farewell letter from my mother. She had apparently thrown it from the train. Kind people—people we will never know—mailed it to us. Every year, I light a candle for my mother on the Jewish High Holy Days.

Piet's language was always very "colorful." Cursing the Germans, he came over to where I was sitting. He had a strong drink in his hand and he said, "I will take the first train to Westerbork tomorrow morning. I'll have the doctor's letter with me, and I will do everything in my power to get your mother out."

I know at the time I was in such shock over my mother's fate that most of what he said was a blur to me. I remember Dina placing a pot of tea on the table. I looked over at Felix and noticed how pale and drawn his face was. He said to me, "This is the greatest tragedy in the history of mankind. Germany was such a cultured nation with the finest universities; it produced famous writers, composers, painters . . . you name it. How can it be that people with doctorate degrees, people who are generally so intelligent, have turned into murderers? How can they commit such brutal crimes without thinking twice about what they're doing?"

For several moments we sat in awkward silence, unable to find the strength to move. Felix continued, "What can be done about Flory's mother? What will become of my mother and Nel and Kurt? What is their fate going to be?" Dina served the hot tea. She said, "Drink your tea and let's get some rest. Everything is in the hands of God. We must trust in Him." She then made the sign of the cross. Piet did the same. Felix and I went up to our room.

Later that night, I searched for the sermon that Mr. Van Dam had given us on our wedding day. I held on to it because I drew comfort from the words. I found the sermon in my purse and read and re-read the words from the Book of Ecclesiastes, which Mr. Van Dam had so eloquently recited at our wedding. Among the verses I read: "God brings everything to pass precisely at its time. There is a time for war, and a time for peace, a time for loving and a time for hating . . . " That night, however, as I lay in bed, I could not find any solace in those words. I preferred to focus on "a time for hating." I hated the Germans and I promised myself that I would never set foot in Germany should we survive. I knew then that the feeling of hate would be with me forever. I spent the rest of the night writing a long letter to my mother, telling her how much I loved her and how I hoped that we would soon be reunited.

Felix and I had a sleepless night. Very early the next morning Piet knocked on our door to tell us he was off to catch the train to Westerbork. I gave him the letter I had written to my mother, which he hid in his shoe. He had to be very careful. After our daily routine of "washing," getting dressed, sneaking out to the W.C., and having something to eat, the front door opened. We could not believe our eyes; Piet had returned. Although we were used to the unexpected, this time we were overcome with fear. Dina and even the children came to our room with Piet; they were all anxious to hear what had happened. Piet told us that there had been a train derailment caused by the resistance. In retaliation, the Germans lined up civilians and shot them. These were the common actions of people who considered themselves part of the "master race."

September 7, 1942

My very beloved children:

This is my farewell letter to you my dear children.

I was unexpectedly taken away Friday night by the German SS and driven in a police car to Amsterdam.

We had to walk in Amsterdam from "Het Westeinde" to "Het Meyerplein," which took us one and one-half hour. I was wearing a thin dress, they did not give me time. I have no money on me, no hat and I miss my glasses.

From Amsterdam we were transported in a freight car to Hooghalen, where we had to walk for two hours at two o'clock in the night, to Camp Westerbork.

Every half-hour large transports from Amsterdam arrive here. Among the people are poor wretches, some of the sick and bewildered, in their eighties. My heart is heavy. I cannot describe the misery that is going on here.

I am very nervous; it is cold and dirty here and there is no way to sleep. We have not had anything to eat since I was deported.

I feel that this will be my last journey; we know what the Germans have in mind for us. We were told that we have to go again on a transport but I don't know where to.

If there is anything left in our home in Rotterdam, maybe the furniture and other household effects can be sold and the proceeds will be for you, my beloved children.

I am sure that God will save you all.

I kiss and embrace you all many, many times. If it is God's will maybe we will see each other again.

Your faithful and loving mother

I translated this letter from Dutch. It was written and thrown from a train by my mother,
Alijda Cohen-Van Beek

We begged Piet to stay home and not attempt to go to Westerbork again; we feared putting his family in danger. He agreed but said that he would try again the next day to catch a train to the camp and deliver the doctor's letter. In the course of the day, as we sat in our room, we heard all kinds of commotion: people from the Resistance Movement coming in and out of the house, talking excitedly.

The next day Piet did go to Westerbork. It was a long day for us, as every day had been, but on this day we were especially anxious. That night Piet returned safe and sound. But the expression on his face told us that my mother's fate had been sealed. Piet learned that she had been put on a transport in the direction of Poland.

About one week later during the morning hours, I clearly remember suddenly hearing my mother's voice calling my name. It was so clear that I even turned around, as if I would find her standing there behind me. In my heart I knew that it was the moment she died.

It was the end of the second week of September 1942.

Chapter 23: Fear—Our Companion

I don't know how I was able to get through the next several days following my mother's deportation. I remember laying on the bed most days trying to trace the moments before her disappearance, minute by minute. What was she feeling? What was she thinking? What would she have said to me? I thought constantly about what she must have gone through. Felix, Piet, and Dina did their best to console me, but my heart was broken. A piece of my soul was gone with my mother with whom I had been so very close.

None of us were able to predict how long the dreadful war would last. I often felt that I would not be able to survive. Too many despicable events had taken place, one after the other. The worst thing was that I believed I could not openly show my grief and become a burden to the brave people who gave us protection and shelter under the most dangerous of circumstances.

Felix's family still lived in the Rubensstraat, and Piet managed to continue to communicate with them. We admired Piet's courage and his kindness; we did not want him to risk being seen too often near their home. Amersfoort was, at that time, a small town where almost everyone knew each other.

One day during the third week in September, we received bad news again. Felix's mother had become ill, and she needed an operation. One of her neighbors had taken her to the local hospital, which, at that time, was forbidden. The Germans did not allow Jews to be treated in the hospitals.

Piet came to our room that morning with the news. He sat down on the bed, waiting for us to calm down. Finally, he said, "You know, if the operation is behind us, the situation for now might be good. She is safe in the hospital and she must stay there as long as she is recuperating. I will contact one of my friends to ensure that she is okay."

Nel and Kurt

Felix and I were devastated. Each time there was another problem to solve, and we were powerless to do anything. Felix asked Piet questions about Nel and Kurt's future; Piet answered, with a concerned yet confident tone, "I must find a hiding place for your sister and Kurt, but they will have to get married first."

I kept thinking, "What a struggle to stay alive . . . is it all worth it?" Before Piet left our room he stood up and said, "I'll come up with something if it's the last thing I do." Then turning to me, he said, "And you, young lady, take it easy. Eventually we will get rid of the Rot-Moffen." This became a slogan and it helped everyone mentally.

When evening came, Piet called for us to come downstairs. Turning to Felix he said, "I know a family down the street. They are a middle-aged couple, good patriots, and very religious *gereformeerd* (translated from the Dutch, Calvinists). I have a feeling that if I go there and speak to them, they might want to help."

Felix said, "Are you sure that it would be safe to let them know that we are here?" "I am convinced," Piet answered. "We have to take that gamble, anyway." The conversation continued, and Piet said, "I will go there tomorrow morning and ask them if they can take your sister and Kurt for a short time, until I have found a permanent place for them." All of us were engrossed in our own thoughts. Finally Felix said, "I see no other way but to go ahead and ask them. All of our lives are hanging by a thin thread anyway. But, Piet, I don't want you in any danger on account of us."

I could understand better now how so many Jewish families had taken their own lives and the lives of their children rather than falling prey to the Germans and facing such slow, morbid destruction. It was because of Piet and Dina that we did not give up. Their courage was unbelievable their demeanor gallant.

At night in bed, Felix and I talked about everything for a long time. He said, "All we can do is pray." I kept looking at the Madonna on the table in our room. Her face reminded me somehow of my mother. It represented serenity, innocence, tranquillity. I don't know what came over me, but I was glad that the statue was there.

Felix was very concerned about the fate of his mother. He looked so forlorn, being unable to stay active as he had since we first knew each other. I knew that the world was not ours any longer. All of us were trapped like animals. I wondered how the Nazis treated Jews in other countries. Whenever we listened to the BBC on the crystal radio, there was never anything mentioned about the fate of the Jews.

The next morning around noon, Piet came to our room. His face was glowing. "I talked to the Van den Hoeven's," he began. "I explained the situation as it is now; then I asked them if they could help to save a young Jewish couple." Piet stopped smoking and then continued. "They were a bit reluctant at first, but they are very religious and they understood that lives have to be saved."

We asked him a few questions about this couple. It turned out that the Van den Hoeven's had four adult children, and they were devout Calvinists. They told Piet that they would speak with their children, who were all old enough to understand the severity of the issue and the importance of

Mr. and Mrs. Van den Hoeven

keeping this a secret. Finally, after a lengthy conversation, Piet stood up, took his pipe in his hand, and said, "I'm going to see Nel and Kurt, and I will also find out how your mother is doing."

After he left us, our tension was high. Felix said, "We must do something to occupy ourselves. It is not good to just sit here the whole day. Maybe we can help Piet or do something with the children." I agreed, but first I had to calm myself; I first needed to know what would happen with Felix's mother and with Nel and Kurt.

That night we went downstairs again after the doors and the curtains were closed. The house had been very quiet. The children's vacation was over and they had gone back to school. On this evening they were already in bed. Dina was preparing tea and Piet was smoking. Piet looked pensive. We prepared ourselves for yet another phase in this ongoing saga of horror and sadness. Decisions were about to be made to save—or lose—three more lives.

Looking at Felix, Piet began: "First of all, your mother is safe in the hospital. The operation went well. They promised to keep her there until it is safe to get her out." I heard Felix utter a sigh of relief, knowing that for the time being, his mother was all right. Piet took a sip of his tea and continued, "I spoke with Nel and Kurt and they agreed to get married. They realize that the time for procrastination is over and that they have to seize the moment for the chance to go into hiding." He added, "And remember, I still have the authorization from Rabbi Tal!"

As we sipped our tea, no one spoke for a while. Piet continued by emphasizing how serious things were. He said, " I am now deeply involved with the resistance. We have contact with England and I have immediate access to all important information. The *Einsatzgruppen* are all over in our country and all other occupied countries. *Einsatzgruppen* translated from the German means "troops," and it specifically applies to those troops designed and trained to kill, such as the SS the SD, and the Gestapo.

Though I knew by now that the Nazis could kill almost nonchalantly, I shuddered. Going into more explicit details, Piet continued, "A number of resistance people, as well as innocent citizens, have been killed. The

Rot-Moffen will soon organize the last round-up of Jews: the old, the sick, the very young, and the babies. All who, in their eyes, are undesirable elements must be wiped out."

It felt like such a long evening. Piet had turned on the crystal—after he had locked all of the doors and made sure the curtains were drawn. We all listened to the BBC and especially what the commentators in England had to say about the development of the war. We knew that it had been a bitter winter in Russia and that the German troops had been forced back into defensive positions near Stalingrad. Felix, who was so well informed about many details of history, spoke: "If Stalingrad can hold out and drive the Germans back, then, in my estimation, the Germans will lose the war eventually. How much longer it will last, we don't know. And how many lives it will cost, who knows."

We became very depressed over the fact that the Japanese, who were allies of the Germans, were occupying the Dutch colonies, named The Netherlands East Indies (now called Indonesia). The tiny crystal permitted us, at least for a few moments, to divert our nightmarish thoughts away from our immediate problems to focus on other parts of the world. A good night's sleep, however, was never within our reach during those years. The grief over my mother's loss kept me awake—it was a grief that would last throughout my life.

Piet had given us the daily newspapers to read, which were censored. The news was always about German victories, as well as the consequences people would face for hiding Jews or Jewish properties. Quite often the words on the front pages of these newspapers read, *Jews are the evil of the world.*

I had left my paper cuttings in the suitcases that were with the Kolkmans. Now I entertained the thought of starting my newspaper clippings again. Indeed, I did continue. About this time Felix began a daily entry in a diary, which later would turn into hundreds of pages. We told Piet about our clippings and our journal entries. He suggested we put them in metal boxes and hide them. How we did this was a story in itself.

There was no access to sleeping pills during those days. I personally spent the vast majority of nights wide awake. Often, both of us had bad nightmares,which interrupted what little sleep we did get. I frequently reached for Mr. Van Dam's wedding sermon, which I had carefully hidden underneath the bed. I honestly tried to make sense of what was happening, but I always ended up with feelings of anger, doubt, uncertainty, and, above all, hatred for the Germans.

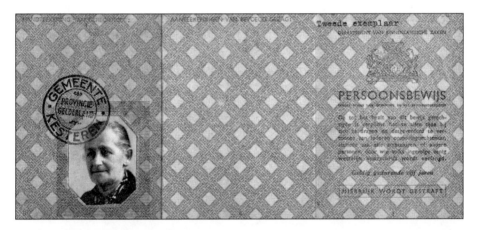

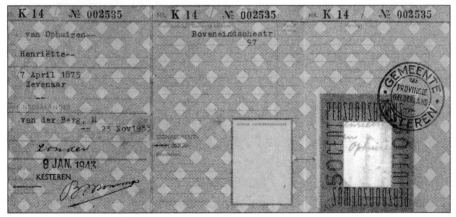

Felix's mother's false identification papers

Chapter 24: A Scale of Life and Death

Now events began to take place quickly, one after the other. We learned from Piet, through his secret connections, that the German police had invaded several Jewish homes to "take inventory," whereby the Jewish families had to fill out lengthy statements regarding their household effects, valuables, rent or mortgage payments, and other details. After they were questioned, they were arrested, because, according to the Germans, they were not supposed to be living where they were anymore, anyway.

The few remaining Jewish families had gone to the Synagogue—what was left of it—and blown the shofar (the ram's horn) to usher in the Jewish New Year 5703. We understood that shortly after our wedding the four Holy Scrolls (the Torahs) had been removed from the Temple by some of the Synagogue members and brought to safety in an undisclosed hiding place.

During this same week Piet told us that Nel and Kurt were married at the home in the Rubensstraat 23; Piet and one of the remaining Jewish members of the Temple officiated. Later this day, Piet sat down and, appearing quite serious, said, "Everything is upside down, thanks to the Nazis." Patting Felix on the back, he continued, "I congratulate you, Jan, on the marriage of your sister. At the same time I must express my sorrow over the loss of Marietje's mother. What a world we live in." Jan, of course, was Felix's "new" name, and Marietje was mine.

As encouraging and courageous as Piet always was, he put his arms around me and said, "I guarantee you that the Rot-Moffen will get what they deserve. In the end we will be free." Then, getting up from the bed he said, "The arrangements have been made with the Van den Hoevens; I will bring Nel and Kurt there tomorrow night, and tomorrow morning I'll go to the hospital and find out how your mother is doing." Though we were relieved to know that Nel and Kurt would be saved, we were nevertheless anxious and tense as we anticipated the future for all of us. We could only hope for a decent ending to this tribulation.

The next morning around noon Piet came to our room to bring us the latest news about Felix's mother. He told us that someone from the resistance had talked to one of the doctors in the hospital, and arrangements had been made to pick up his mother on a certain evening during the third week of September. She, too, would go into hiding. Piet informed us that the same night that he checked on Felix's mother, Nel and Kurt had been safely escorted to the Van den Hoeven family home; they had left everything behind in the Rubensstraat. Although the news about Felix's family was good, I still had not gotten over the trauma of what had happened to my mother.

Felix and I also wondered what had happened to my Aunt and Uncle de Haas, who lived in Rotterdam. And, of course, we had no idea where my brothers and sister were. We knew from Piet that my brother's neighbors had taken over my brother's business, but no one knew a thing about their whereabouts. That night in the Brandsen's sitting room, Piet said, "You know, I have to go to Rotterdam next week to meet people from the resistance. Give me the address of your family and I will try to get some information for you."

There was much to discuss during the evenings we could leave our room and join Dina and Piet downstairs. During these evenings, we again felt like human beings and not like caged animals. We discussed a possible hiding place for Felix's mother, how her recovery was progressing, and how she would endure hiding for an undetermined period of time. Would she be able to cope? How would she handle the language barrier? Piet assured us that there was a place where she could hide and reminded us that we still had a week to sort out the details.

Dina always remained silent during these intense discussions. It was evident that she adored her husband, and we sensed that whatever Piet proposed, whatever plans he suggested, were always fine with her. She completely trusted his judgment in any circumstance.

Piet often spoke freely about the Resistance Movement. We were, at times, concerned about the danger, yet we felt that he knew what he was doing and how far he could go without putting himself and his family at risk.

In spite of the time he spent in the resistance and at work, Piet managed to build a small hiding place in our room underneath the staircase. I prayed we would never be forced to use it. Piet told us of his plans to build more hiding places downstairs in case someone who was not involved with the resistance—and not sympathetic to the cause—should come into the house unexpectedly. He talked about eventually building an air raid shelter in the yard, since there were more and more air raids as the war escalated.

Piet was a most ingenious person, keenly intelligent, and a hard worker. He would never mince words; he was too sincere and courageous. We felt truly blessed to have met him and his family. It was difficult for us to shake the feeling that we were imposing on these people, opening them up to great danger.

A few days passed when Piet told us that his trip to Rotterdam was set for the next morning. He had also set a date with the hospital to pick up Felix's mother. For the time being, until a more "permanent" hiding place could be found, she would stay with the Van den Hoevens.

Piet left early the next morning, letting us know that he would be back in the afternoon and that he would definitely inquire about my family while he was in Rotterdam. At around three o'clock in the afternoon that day we heard Piet's voice. He immediately ran into our room; he looked absolutely stunned. He said, "Jan, I found your mother on the street. I took her to the Van den Hoevens." Dina also ran up to our room. All of us were flabbergasted.

What had happened, we learned, was that there was an unexpected razzia by the Germans at the hospital. The doctors and hospital staff— thinking they would save Felix's mother's life—let her go into the streets.

Piet, on his way home from Rotterdam, decided to take a different route home from the railroad station than he usually took. He could not explain his reasons why; it was more impulse than anything else. Although he had gone his familiar way home from the railroad station hundreds of times, on this particular day something prompted him to try another route. On his way home he came upon an elderly woman who had a familiar face. It was, of course, Felix's mother. She was sitting on the curb, crying and praying that she would find help. She had wandered, pushing her frail body for blocks, not knowing where to go or what to do. She was still weak from her operation.

Piet immediately took her away from the main streets and brought her to the Van den Hoevens. If ever a true miracle happened, it was on this day. It could not be explained any other way than a guardian angel watching over her. It was mind-boggling!

After Piet told us the details, we stood there silent for quite some time. Finally Piet said, "You two must take in some fresh air. Take some deep breaths." He opened the door to the small balcony, and as I counted my breaths—one, two three, inhale—I sensed that the three of us were also trying to breathe in some understanding of the magnitude of what had taken place that day. Piet broke the silence by lighting another cigarette. He said, "I have to rush off again, but I'll see you tonight, downstairs. I have some new information for you, Marietje. In the meantime, try to relax." I interrupted him, "But Piet, can't you tell me now?" But he insisted that we would talk later, after he returned.

When evening came, Dina called us to come downstairs. We sat around the table, as usual, Dina busy with preparing and serving a surrogate tea, Piet in his lazy chair, smoking. Piet began, "We have to be grateful that your mother is safe, Jan. But now I have some bad news for you, Marietje." Again, I felt that horrible feeling in the pit of my stomach. Piet continued, "I went to the address you gave me of your Aunt and Uncle de Haas; no one was there. I then inquired at a neighbor's home. They told me that your family had received the summons to go to the train station to be relocated— well, you know, as the Germans call it. It sounds better than openly saying 'to send them to the death camps.' The neighbors were adamant to help your family find hiding places, but your uncle refused to bother anyone or to be the cause of their deaths, so he went voluntarily to the train station. He had said good-bye to his family, neighbors, and friends."

As Piet spoke, I kept thinking that it would have been better if we had drowned in the North Sea; we would have been spared this endless heartache. We had no choice now but to deal the best we could with these awful circumstances. I asked Piet, "What happened to my Aunt Sien and my cousin Jaap?" He told me that no one knew their whereabouts; the neighbors hoped they were hiding somewhere. Piet added, I believe to console us, "I know that your aunt and uncle in the Van Dieststraat are still okay. I have my connections; they will keep me up-to-date."

Later, upstairs in our room, Felix and I said to each other, "What next?" I was unable to fall asleep, and my thoughts became philosophical. I thought, "Every second of time that passes will never come back; each moment is gone forever. How will the next moments be? Will we be dead or alive? All of us were just a second in history."

My uncle, Ephraim de Haas, a famous chessmaster

WORKING FOR THE RESISTANCE

Chapter 25: The Room Upstairs

There was no way we could be in direct contact with Felix's family, nor could Piet be seen at the Van den Hoevens'; it would have provoked suspicion. Piet had said to us that he would drop by the Van den Hoeven's home on occasion during the evenings so it would look like a casual visit. The Van den Hoevens, fearing serious repercussions, hinted that they did not want much contact with Piet, since they had three Jewish people hiding in their home.

The resistance had also found a hiding place for Kurt's mother. She was with an older couple somewhere near a small town called Baarn. It was near a place where the exiled queen had lived in her palace. Felix asked Piet how Kurt's mother would manage without knowing a word of Dutch. Piet joked, "Well, it might be a good thing because now she cannot get into trouble with them!" I had met Kurt's mother on only a few occasions. She seemed to be a friendly, elderly woman. We knew she was a diabetic and our concern was how she would manage without any medication.

None of us knew, from a medical perspective, how serious her condition was. We heard from time to time that she was doing all right. Perhaps the fact that there was not enough food available automatically kept her on a diet; this may have stabilized her illness. She lived through the war, but unfortunately, a few months after the liberation, she passed away.

At night Felix and I could leave our room and go downstairs—after Dina called to us with her customary "the coast is clear." We had so much to discuss. Most of these evenings the children were already asleep. It was during one of these nights that Piet said to us, "I was at the

Van den Hoevens; everyone is okay, and I have a message for both of you from your mother. Your family wishes you a happy New Year, and your mother wants you to observe the Atonement Day (the Yom Kippur High Holy Day). She said it is around this time."

I became extremely upset and angry. In fact, I remember this episode as if it were just yesterday. Although I tried to keep my anger under control, I blurted out, "What should we atone for! God should atone for what He does to His people!" How could we have a happy New Year with my mother gone, far away in a concentration camp, who knew where? I ended my tirade by saying, "I won't hear about it, and I have no message back."

An awkward silence filled the air. As fate would have it, an air raid siren began to blare, and we heard planes flying low overhead. There was a great deal of noise up in the air. After a long, tense few minutes, the "all clear" signal blew and, much to my relief, the High Holy Day conversation was over. It was not mentioned again that evening. I had intended to be a good and dedicated wife to Felix, but the circumstances under which we found ourselves did not allow this.

I had mentioned to Piet that I knew how to type, a skill I had learned at the practical language school in Rotterdam. Piet was elated to hear this and said he would mention it to *Het Parool*, the newspaper of the Resistance Movement. It was one of the most important underground newspapers during the war years. *Het Parool* was secretly distributed among the most trustworthy and patriotic citizens. The newspaper contained, among other things, the latest news from the BBC, information on the Germans' current strategies, and crimes the Nazis committed against the Dutch people.

The winter had already set in and food became even more scarce. Piet had indicated that the resistance was very busy with falsifying food coupons. One evening he said to us, "If Marietje can type, it would be a big help. We have lists of people who are hiding Jewish people; they urgently need extra coupons; we also help families of the resistance workers." I replied that I would be more than happy to help; Felix said he would take the administration of this project on himself. Piet said, "I am going to speak with the people from *Het Parool*. They will not betray me for hiding Jewish people in my home."

For a while I had this strange premonition that a calamity would befall us again. I talked to Felix about it, but he explained, as was his philosophy, we were "branded" anyway, so we might as well make ourselves useful in any way we could. I agreed with him, but I felt uncomfortable that people would know where we were. Of course I was also concerned about the safety of the Brandsen family.

During this time, in the winter of 1942, Felix began to feel deep pain in his shoulder and arm. He could not sleep at night, and, of course, he could not visit a doctor for his condition. At first, Felix did not want to mention his discomfort to Dina and Piet. However, as intuitive as Piet was, he began to sense that something was wrong with Felix. Finally, Felix told them of his pain. Dina said, "I know of a remedy; it is an old Dutch recipe and it always helps. Believe it or not, it is petroleum."

In order to get some petroleum, Piet had to lie and say that it was he who had the pain in his shoulder and arm. In those days, one had to think through everything—and every lie—to protect oneself. Shortly thereafter, Piet came home with a container of petroleum, and Felix started his treatment immediately. Within a week, the pains disappeared! Needless to say, the treatment smelled awful. Even Opa mumbled about the odor and accused the "darned Belzen" of bringing gasoline into the house.

Piet, Dina, Felix, and I listened every day to the forbidden crystal. Before we turned it on, we had to lock all of the doors and be sure that not a bit of light shone through the windows to the outside of the house. The Germans were known to shoot into homes that did not completely follow the rules of the blackout times.

We closely followed the battle of Stalingrad; this was, for us, the turning point. The Germans had already survived a horribly cold winter in Russia, and another winter was approaching. Russia was the determining factor for us at that time. Our anxiety worked overtime as the tension grew; we did not want to see the Germans gain control of Russian oil fields, which were located in Siberia and in the Caucasian Mountains. The war seemed to go on forever!

As we were waiting to see if we could help and work for the resistance, Felix and I made ourselves as useful as possible. We had to be extremely careful not to make any noise; we were constantly on our guard because during the day we could hear people coming in and out of the house.

The girls were wonderful. Even though they always brought play-mates home, they instinctively knew what to do and what not to do, with us hiding upstairs. Meanwhile, winter set in. The days were short and darkness fell in the afternoon. When the children's playmates left, the girls always came upstairs where I helped them with their homework and catechism or played games with them. After they had gone to bed, I helped Dina with sewing and mending.

During the days, Felix worked on his diary or he polished shoes. At night he listened to the tiny crystal with Piet; afterward they often had a lengthy conversation about the war. The days were extremely difficult for us. As was the custom in Holland, people would take great care of keeping the streets in front of their homes clean by scrubbing them with soap and hot water. At times it would take Dina a great deal of the morning hours to complete this ritual, because it also included talking with neighbors. This, I know, was a good thing because any suspicion was avoided.

I prayed a lot during those days. I prayed that we would not be dis-covered and that no harm would befall the family Brandsen on account of our being there. I prayed that we would not get sick. But mostly I prayed for my mother that a miracle would happen and we would be reunited again. We hadn't the faintest idea where my siblings were. Because I could not fathom a God who would allow the Jewish people to be annihilated, I prayed to no one in particular. I simply addressed my prayers "to whom it may concern," which included God anyhow.

Chapter 26: *Het Parool:* Helping the Cause

Piet kept busy building hiding places. He was working on another one downstairs in the hallway near the kitchen, in a room that had been a storage area that most Dutch homes were equipped with. As was the custom in Holland, people used these spaces for preserving vegetables and other homemade foods. Building a hiding place here was a brilliant idea because one could quickly enter it from the right or the left entrance. Coming from the yard or the kitchen, we could disappear into this hiding place should a neighbor come to the front door. If we were on the staircase and the doorbell rang, then we could enter the hiding place from the right. Piet had also made a double door for this hideout; it was larger than the one in our bedroom upstairs. Both hiding places were frightening; we could hardly stand being in either one since little air could come in from the outside.

Piet was also busy making an electrical connection leading from the front entrance of the home to our room. In case of danger, someone could push a button downstairs and a red light would go on in our room, indicating that we must immediately hide. By the end of October, Piet had completed all of these security measures.

In the meantime we kept ourselves as busy as was possible. We were working on a dollhouse for the children with what little material was available. It was a tedious job, but seeing the joy on the girls' faces, and the enthusiasm with which they ran up to our room after school each day was the greatest reward we could ask for.

One evening Piet came home with a suitcase in which he had hidden a typewriter. He turned to me and said, "Marietje, I'll bring it upstairs and then you can try it out. But one of the *Parool* people wants to come and make sure that all hiding places are in order, insisting that we have a rehearsal of what to do in case of an emergency before we start working for them. I will be honest with you—there is danger connected to the work here." Danger was no stranger to us; we always felt as if our lives were in peril. Felix was marvelous in this respect. He said to Piet, "One way or the other, I will fight till death, and whatever I can do for the cause, I will. It is an honor to participate."

The next evening after the children had gone to bed, the four of us went upstairs to our room to practice. The plan was for Piet to push the button that was connected to the light in our room. As soon as we saw the red light go on, we were to quickly and very quietly sneak into our hiding place. The red light appeared and in we went. Piet had done such a superb job. With great ingenuity, he had designed a lock on the inside of the small compartment in our room; he had also made a second door so that the entrance had double doors. We executed the practice exactly as planned, but once I was inside the compartment I was struck by a terrible attack of claustrophobia. I could not wait to get out. What would happen if we really had to hide this way?

Late one evening a person from the resistance came to Piet's home. He brought with him a small suitcase filled with lists of names, food coupons, documents and papers from *Het Parool*. This man did not mince words. He said, "I am Jeroen." It was not his real name, of course. He shook hands with us, then continued, "I want to see the layout and the safety devices." First, we all went upstairs while Piet was explaining the details of our emergency plan. Jeroen then said to Piet, "She must not type while you have people downstairs. No sound must be heard, ever." After Jeroen inspected our hiding place upstairs, we went downstairs so he could see the other hiding place. In this one, we were able to stand up while inside.

Dina, always hospitable, offered us all some tea. Jeroen thanked her politely but declined. He preferred to spend time discussing more details. He admonished us to keep the secret papers in the hiding place as much as possible and to only take out the lists that needed to be typed. Felix was to do all of the administration, and Piet would be in direct contact with the resistance as far as our work was concerned. Jeroen stayed for a while longer, asking about the children, the neighbors, Opa, and any visitors. After he left, we carefully closed all doors and made sure all were locked up. Then we went to bed.

The next morning we started to work on the assignment. I could type pretty quickly, but all the while I had to listen for people downstairs. If so, I had to stop typing immediately; I always had to be on guard. The noise of my typewriter luckily droned out the loud clang of the clock. Unfortunately, during my many sleepless nights, the noise of that clock went straight to my nerves.

The food coupons were masterly counterfeited. They were distributed to families who had people in hiding, to families of the resistance workers, and to all who needed food, which was scarce. Our assignment was to make lists with the names of people who needed to receive the coupons: how many were to be given out, the names of the people, dates. The coupons had to be numbered so that accurate records could be kept. Piet was responsible for the distribution of these coupons. We also had to keep records of documents and type duplicates of information, as well as articles for *Het Parool.* We realized how very dangerous this work was, and we were mostly concerned for Piet.

We soon got the hang of it, and the days went by a bit more quickly. On Sundays, the whole family went to church, leaving Felix and me alone with Opa. We always carefully locked all of the doors and hoped that Opa would not have to go to the WC and, therefore, unlock the kitchen door.

Christmas had come and gone, and as the new year 1943 began, the war raced on. Now the Americans were deeply involved. One evening, in the first week of February, while Dina and I were mending socks and the two men were listening to the crystal, Piet and Felix suddenly began to shout jubilantly. A Russian general had surrounded Hitler's sixth army and destroyed it. The German General von Paulus surrendered, and the Germans were driven out. Piet and Felix believed this was the turning point of Hitler's war.

There was also bad news: our dear friend Kolkman had been shot and killed by the Nazis during a sabotage attempt by the resistance workers, which he was a part of. He was only in his mid-thirties; all of us were deeply saddened by this terrible news, and we hoped that his wife and two children would be able to cope with the loss.

One night, not long after this, Felix developed a terrible toothache. At first we gave him aspirin, but as the days wore on, the toothache became worse. He was clearly in agony, and we could see how much he suffered; at times he was even doubled over in pain. Piet and Dina realized that professional help was needed. Piet said, "I know a physician who is connected with the resistance. I'll ask Jeroen if I can talk to him."

The next day an arrangement was made, and Piet went to see the doctor. When he returned home, he came to our room and said, "There is no other way but to go and see a dentist. The doctor explained to me that the problem may develop into an infection; he cannot do anything about it." Turning to Felix Piet added, "My friends in the resistance will find a good, patriotic dentist whom we can trust." The same evening, Jeroen came to the house with the name of a reliable dentist who, unfortunately, lived quite far from Piet's home. We had a decision to make: take the chance of Felix becoming very sick, or take the risk of going to this dentist. We decided that the latter was better.

So one evening, after all had been arranged for us, the three of us—Piet, Felix, and I—set off in the dark to the dentist's office. As in the past, Piet walked ahead, with the two of us following him. It was a walk of at least forty-five minutes or more, and each minute seemed like hours. There were no back streets to take; each step was a grave risk. That evening is engraved in my mind as if it were just yesterday. When we arrived, the dentist was waiting for us. Piet introduced us and we all shook hands. The dentist appeared to be quite nervous and so, of course, were we. Thank goodness we had not met any German soldiers on the way! But there were always Nazi collaborators looking about, and we had to be very cautious.

The dentist said, "I better not turn on the lights; one never knows. I can work by candlelight." Then turning to Piet and me, he said, "You two, please wait in the other room." He then lit some candles, and while Piet and I waited in another room, he worked on Felix. It took a long time, but finally Felix emerged minus one tooth, which the doctor had extracted. The doctor said, "Here are the medications that you must take as prescribed." We wanted to pay him for his services, but he refused. We shook hands again with him, and he wished the three of us good luck. He then said, "Remember, I have never seen you people, ever, in my life."

It had gotten quite late and our next worry was walking the same distance home. I remember the tension; Felix with bloody cotton in his mouth; planes flying overhead; and Piet walking ahead of us. A guardian angel must have watched over us again because finally we returned home safely, with Dina anxiously waiting for us with the customary tea ("surrogate" tea, by now). The medication that the dentist had given Felix worked, and in a few days he felt much better.

The air raids became more and more frequent. The British and the Germans frequently fought it out above our heads. It was time to build an air raid shelter, Piet told us. Being an expert contractor, Piet knew exactly what to do and how to build one. Within a month he completed a shelter with water, food, and household items stored inside. He also made a contraption in the yard where we could hide Felix's diaries and my newspaper clippings, which were stored in metal boxes. He and Dina agreed that we should keep all documents because in the event that we should survive this ordeal, we could easily dig up the valuable papers. If not us, then someone would. We knew they had to be saved—they were history.

My thoughts were always with my mother, and my heart broke when I read the letter that she had thrown out of the train, and which, by some miracle, reached me. There was no way to gain personal contact with my aunt and uncle, who still lived in the van Dieststraat. We heard that Felix's family at the Van den Hoevens' were doing fairly well, but everyone was scattered about or in concentration camps.

As spring began, we learned that my aunt and uncle had been deported; they were forced to leave their beloved Amersfoort on April 15, 1943. They had been born and raised there and happily lived with my grandparents. Their destination had been—as we later learned—Sobibor and the gas chambers.

Chapter 27: Food for Thought

As a special note to this testimonial of our survival of the Holocaust, I want to mention that at the time I am currently describing, we had no idea what the fate was of those who had been deported. Though we understood that the Germans were malicious and had nothing good planned for those who ended up in concentration camps, we had no concept of what had really happened to these poor people. Our understanding began to heighten at the end of 1943. Jeroen stopped by one evening and while he and Piet were talking in the hallway, I overheard him mention the words "gas chamber." The context of the conversation was not understood by us; however, we kept thinking about what Jeroen had meant. Because our minds could not perceive such evil, we dismissed the words from our thoughts.

Though I knew deep in my heart that neither my mother nor my other loved ones would be able to survive in a concentration camp for a long time, I still carried a flicker of hope that perhaps—against all odds—a miracle could happen and I would see my mother again.

And so, amidst hope, doubt, fear and worry, the weeks and months went by while we fervently worked with Piet for "The Cause." Felix and I worked faithfully; I at the typing and Felix at the administrating, both of us always on alert for strangers downstairs. Food became scarce. Somehow, Piet and Dina knew how to buy what I called snakes better known as eel. After the doors were locked and the curtains drawn, we helped them prepare the eel by cutting off their heads. The eel still wriggled around in the sink, even headless. I hated looking at them; it gave me the shivers. But Dina had a way of preparing them, and when dinner was served, I diverted my thoughts from the headless creatures and bravely ate my meal.

Around the beginning of June 1943, the general health condition of the Dutch people became quite bad. The Germans were sending large food supplies to Germany to feed their own people. It was around this time that the majority of the Dutch physicians sent a petition to Seyss-Inquart, still the head of the occupation troops in Holland. The petition was signed by hundreds of physicians. It was quite a courageous deed, considering the hateful mentality of the Nazis.

The petition appeared in the newspapers, and it was also distributed among people in the resistance. The document consisted of two pages, beautifully written in the Dutch language. Among other things, it stated that because of the scarcity of food, the spread of tuberculosis had become serious. Malnutrition among the Dutch was causing many deaths. The petition also mentioned the Treaty of 1907, executed in the Hague, clearly stating that no occupied country would suffer starvation on account of occupational troops. Piet gave us a copy of this document, which Felix immediately put in our secret metal box; thus, it was preserved for history. At the end of the letter the physicians appealed to the conscience of Seyss-Inquart. The result was terrible. A great number of the physicians who signed the petition were deported to Germany, never to be heard from again.

One evening when the four of us were sitting together, Felix said, "You know, I just got an idea. Last year, I saved for my cousins in Rotterdam—who are now safely in South America—all their valuable household effects, art and furniture. Mr. Loos is the man who helped me retrieve these things with his moving truck. Together, we brought all of these items to his home. He promised to hide everything in his attic, where it is safe. I remember what a dangerous mission that had been! If I had left these goods in Rotterdam, I am sure the Germans would have found the house and emptied it by now. I'm convinced that Mr. Loos is a good patriotic citizen. He lives right near here. The time has come to get some extra food, and I'm willing to go to him and take some of the valuables out so that we can exchange it with the farmers for extra food. What do you think, Piet?"

Piet and Dina just nodded. That evening, a lot of things were discussed. Although Felix did not want to bring any danger to Piet and his family, he genuinely was eager to go to Mr. Loos' house himself at night to retrieve some of the things he thought that farmers would swap for food. As the evening progressed, so did our talks and our worries. Food was imperative to stay alive. The family Van den Hoeven now had five Jewish people in their home. They had taken in Kurt' s mother, who had to move from her original hiding place in Baarn because of the elderly couple's illness. The family Van den Hoeven had graciously offered to take her in, as well as another Jewish person. We later learned that this other person was rarely seen; she spent day and night in her hiding place upstairs.

All in all, there were now fourteen people who needed food. Though Piet was at first hesitant that Felix should go, the pros and cons were thoroughly discussed. If Piet should go, then Mr. Loos might become suspicious. But if Felix went, Mr. Loos would not get to know where Felix resided. And so, the decision was that Felix would go. The next evening Felix left on Piet's bike. He went through the backyard, into the alley, and around the block to Mr. Loos' home. Before Felix left, Piet said to him, "I'll give you an hour. If you are not back by then, I will start looking for you. Be sure to have your papers with you."

The tension was great. I kept thinking, "What if . . . what if . . . " and attaching horrible things to the end of those sentences, imagining Felix coming into all kinds of danger. Dina had made the sign of the cross when Felix left, as was her habit in dangerous situations. Somehow, that act had given me a kind of reassurance, which I could not explain at the time.

Within less than an hour Felix returned safe and sound, carrying a number of paintings and clothes. What a relief it was to see him! He told us that he had rung the bell at Mr. Loos' home, and when Mr. Loos answered the door he recognized Felix immediately. He guided Felix to the attic, never asking any questions.

The day before, Piet had made contact with some of the farmers living in Hoogland, a nearby village where they raised their crops. Our plan seemed to be working out well, and the next day Piet left early on his bike to Hoogland to exchange some items for food. Although the value of the paintings and the art greatly exceeded not only the cost of the food but also the farmers' knowledge of their value, the food, to us, was more precious.

And so Felix went to Mr. Loos' from time to time, after which Piet exchanged the items for food for the Van den Hoevens and the Brandsens. We were grateful that all went well, while the food sustained all of us.

One day, Piet came home with two large bags of beans. They appeared as gold in our eyes! It was midsummer, and Piet suggested that the beans should be laid out on our balcony to dry. The weather was great! Dina helped to spread out the beans in their full glory. It was a sight to behold. There were enough beans to share with two families.

The next morning we suddenly heard a loud noise. I ran toward the balcony shouting, "Oh, the beans! It must be raining." Quickly opening the door, I saw there was no rain. It was Opa, who had thrown the contents of his chamber pot out of his window and onto the precious beans. We ran downstairs with great excitement, telling Dina and Piet what had happened. At first Piet made a joke of it, saying, "Oh, that Opa and his secret transmitters!" After they had come upstairs to see the mess, Piet said, "We can still eat them but not as they are now. We have to wash them off."

The next few hours were spent running up and down the stairs with buckets of water, trying to undo Opa's insolence. After all that, Piet motioned to Dina, saying, "Cook the beans a bit longer so that all of the germs are gone." Then he added, "You know what . . . cook them along with the eels. What's the difference, everything goes into one stomach anyway!"

I had always been extremely health conscious, but between the beans and the eels, and the tulip bulbs we occasionally had to eat, I rapidly lost weight. However, we were grateful for everything: for the kind Brandsen family, for the love and understanding they showed us, and for the Van den Hoeven family who so graciously sheltered Felix's family. Before each meal I said a silent prayer of thanks in my own way.

QUO VADIS?

Chapter 28: The Madonna

The air raid shelter in the backyard was well used because much fighting went on in the skies above us, while sirens blasted day and night. The Americans had begun their bombing by day over the occupied territories; unfortunately at times, they missed their targets and hit civilians. Many lives were lost. I became terrified every time I heard planes fly overhead. I would lose all composure, begin shaking and crying, and run in panic toward the air raid shelter. At times, Felix became impatient with me. He said, "Let's be happy that the Americans are here; they are helping us to become free again."

One day, as the sirens began to blast again and the planes roared overhead, we all ran into the shelter. Suddenly, the neighbors next door, the family Kerkhof, also came running in. We all huddled together and after the "all clear" signal had sounded, we left the shelter. As Mrs. Kerkhof took a look at Felix and me, Dina said, "These are two relatives from Belgium." With a good-natured gesture of her hand, Mrs. Kerkhof said, "Don't worry; everything is safe with us." At that time, I paid no attention to what she meant by that statement. I could think of nothing but the bombings. I left everything to fate.

While the Americans bombed during the day, the British bombed during the night. Yet the buzzing of their airplanes flying over to Germany was a welcome sound. Our hearts went out to the brave pilots from America and Britain. Piet, at this time, was totally immersed in the resistance. He assisted pilots whose planes had been shot down.

The Germans continued to issue new ordinances and laws that further terrorized the lives of all Dutch people. The Nazis instituted a "Compulsory Work Program," requiring all citizens to work in Germany for the German war effort. Those who could not prove that they completed this work program were prevented from continuing their studies or their jobs. They also were not allowed to get food. Consequently, many people were left without income, nor could they buy food or obtain food coupons.

Men between the ages of twenty-two and forty were requisitioned to report to the German authorities, who would then transport them to Germany. Those men who were able to find hiding places disappeared. Piet reported that there were few men seen on the streets anymore; Dina begged Piet to be careful during the day. He was thirty-eight years old—a prime age to be picked up by the Germans and deported. Ordinances always appeared with the typical German efficiency, along with the customary threats in case of noncompliance.

The Germans also ordered all Dutch to turn in their bank notes of one thousand and five hundred Dutch guilders. Dina and I were perplexed as to why all this. Piet and Felix understood the politics of the Germans better. They explained to us that most probably the Germans wanted to prevent people from fleeing the country with large sums of money.

Worst of all were the announcements in the newspapers—sadistically summed up reports of the executions of Dutch citizens. One of my February 2, 1943, newspaper clippings from The Hague reads as follows in German:

> *Der Hohere SS und Polizeifuhrer Nordwest und Generalkommisar fur das Sicherheitswesen get. Rauter SS Gruppenfuhrer und General-leutnant der Polizei, Macht Bekannt . . .*

Translated, this means, "The highest SS and police commander of the Northwest [Holland] and the General for the Commissioner of the Security Department, Rauter, announce the following. . ." Then followed the names, ages, and residences of people who were executed by the

Germans. The Germans actually referred to them as "communist-inspired agitators."

The orders were always signed by Rauter (Hanns Albin Rauter), an Austrian SS officer who was assigned as Heinrich Himmler's principal representative in the Netherlands in 1940 for the purpose of exterminating the Dutch Jews. Rauter committed the most heinous crimes in Holland for which he was promoted to the highest police rank as executor to the "final solution" by Himmler. Himmler, of course, was one of Hitler's lieutenants and called "The Butcher of Europe's Jewry." Rauter regarded the extermination of the Jews as a glorious chapter in Germany's history. After the war, he was sentenced to death by a Dutch court and executed in 1949. His boss, Himmler, was captured by the British in 1945; he committed suicide that same year.

In that same year, 1943, the Germans ordered the closure of theaters, restaurants, and any business they did not deem valuable to their cause. In spite of the dismal circumstances, we all looked forward to the evenings when we gathered to listen to the BBC. By listening to the crystal radio we learned that many German cities such as Essen, Munchen, and Berlin had been heavily bombed by the Allies; the cities of Wilhelms and Cuxhaven were totally destroyed. Despite all this, the Germans kept bragging in the newspapers about their victories.

While the Germans had designed their Luftwaffe (air force), to work closely with ground forces in their Blitzkrieg (lightning war), the Allies developed bombers that could fly long distances. They could make daily raids over Europe.

In May of 1943, we found a most unusual piece of news in the papers. The Germans had accused a Jewish person, a chemicals specialist living in London, of being guilty of a terrorist attack on the dams in Germany. Apparently, this air bombing had done so much damage that the Nazis swore that in retaliation they would punish all Jewish people who were still alive.

One evening in July, while we were sitting together, Dina served tea with cookies. I had not seen the cookies before and noticing my puzzled look, Dina said, "Tonight is special." She then looked at Piet, who walked to the serre (sitting room), returning with a flower pot. He came over to Felix and me and with his customary humor sang "Happy Anniversary." He then handed me the flowers.

It was July 9, 1943, our wedding anniversary, which we both had apparently forgotten. Piet gave me a hug, shook hands with Felix, then reaching into his pockets he removed a letter and handed it to us. It was from Felix's family at the Van den Hoevens. I still have both letters in my possession. One was from Nel and Kurt and the other from Felix's mother, who wrote to us in beautiful German "Buchstaben," a special style of written letters. They congratulated us on our one-year anniversary. We were very touched by the flowers, the cookies, and the letters, and we thanked the Brandsens for making the day so special for us under such difficult circumstances.

Piet reported that our family was fine. He had talked to Mr. and Mrs. Van den Hoeven who told him that Felix's mother carried her prayer book with her everywhere and prayed constantly. Even when bombs were flying over-head and everyone huddled together downstairs, Felix's mother's trust in her faith was so strong that she stayed in her room and continued to pray.

For us, it had been a continuous nightmare since 1939. My thoughts were always with my darling mother and siblings. Where could they be? And would we ever see them again?

In the meantime, Felix and I continued typing, sorting, and filing—in general, helping Piet in the resistance. I clearly remember one day in particular. It was late in the afternoon. Autumn had set in and the days grew short. Although we knew better, we had papers spread about the table in our bedroom. This could have been dangerous.

The Madonna was on the table amidst all of the mess. On this day, as Felix and I worked away, Piet and Jeroen came up to our room. Suddenly Piet took the Madonna away, saying, "You don't need this here; I'll take her downstairs so that you have more space." I don't know what came over me, but I panicked and blurted out, "No, no—I want to keep her here." The three men looked absolutely puzzled, especially Felix. Jeroen said good-naturedly, "Let her have it." Piet put the statue back on the table. I did not dare look at Felix.

Later that night I tried to think about it. My mind had become so twisted during those years! Most likely, I had connected the Madonna with my mother's image. Later in bed, Felix and I talked about the incident. Felix said, "Everything is in the hands of God." We kissed and wished each other many more anniversaries in the hope that there would someday be an end to the atrocities committed by the Nazis.

My thoughts turned to our wedding day, so full of fear and mixed emotions. I reached for Mr. Van Dam's speech again. It had ended with the words of Job: "In His hand is every living soul, and the breath of all mankind." I finally fell asleep.

Chapter 29: The Night of the Demons

The hardships that everyone suffered during that long war became unbearable at times. The devious ordinances from the occupying forces affected every household. Farmers, especially, were severely affected. The Germans needed horses, cows, chickens, and other livestock, which they confiscated. In many instances, they also took the farmhands, who were then transported to Germany to work. Later, we learned that a number of those poor victims were never heard from again. People who drove trucks for commercial purposes had to obtain applications to get permits for gasoline. They had to apply in person to the offices of German authorities and fill out endless forms. Many did not want to go; those who were fortunate enough to find hiding places disappeared.

Since 1942, the population had to deal with all kinds of substitutes for most edible items. For example, there were surrogates for tea, coffee, and tobacco. Every household was allotted only a small amount of foods—truly minimal portions. For instance, one was allowed no more than two hundred fifty grams of bread and ten grams of flour. Sugar and butter or margarine were almost unobtainable. One-fourth of a liter of lowfat milk had to be sufficient for a family with children. One kilo of potatoes was a feast. Fish was free but only limited kinds.

Many families ran out of linens, blankets, and underwear. Shoes were no longer available, which was a tragedy for growing children. Felix learned how to patch up shoes with wooden soles for the four children. He became quite good at it, and it kept him busy. I had not seen stockings for three years and was always wearing my woolen knee highs. As a result of the lack of clothing, as well as the constant bombing, children could no longer go to school.

The beautiful carillons of the churches' belltowers were confiscated and sent to Germany to be made into weapons. The defenses that the Germans had made along the coast caused hundreds, if not thousands, of people to evacuate their homes.

Because of the blackout, which had to be strictly observed, people often drowned in the many rivers and canals of the country. The farmers became besieged by the civilian population who tried to exchange their meager possessions for food. People needed their bikes to go to the countrysides, but the bikes now had wooden wheels, which made a terrible noise. Rubber tires did not exist any longer.

At times, Dina and I felt like falling apart, but Piet and Felix kept up the good spirit, which was necessary for our daily struggle. Each time I heard the planes coming I became panicky. Felix said, "These are forerunners for the liberation. Be glad they are here." I was not listening; I just ran and ran. Piet consoled me and said, "You have to grit your teeth and persevere. Holland shall be free!"

The bombings sometimes took place on Sundays, when the Allied forces knew people would not be working. They wanted to avoid hitting civilians. The Brandsen family bravely went to church. When the sirens began to blast, there was not much time to go to the attic and get Opa. We tried many times to get him downstairs, but he was not aware of what was going on and could barely hear. He was as deaf as a post.

Piet was fearless; he had nerves of steel. We were fascinated as we listened to his descriptions of the many heroic deeds of the brave people of the resistance throughout the country. As we read about it in *Het Parool.* I often became quite anxious about the consequences, should any information leak out. I hung on to Felix for strength, especially when he uttered with confidence, "We have come so far now, we must go through with it. We must share our portion and do our part against the enemy."

And so the year 1943 dragged on. Christmas had passed and a new year dawned on us. When Piet sneaked to the Van den Hoevens' now and then, we exchanged letters with Felix's family. My mother-in-law was blessed with a beautiful style of writing. She had sent good wishes to us in September for Rosh Hashana, for Hanukkah, and for the secular year 1944. We always guessed about the actual dates for the Jewish holidays, but we figured that September must be the Jewish New Year and Yom Kippur. Around Christmas it must be Hanukkah. Felix would remind me of these festivals, but as for myself during these years, they did not mean anything to me.

During the last six months of 1943, Piet often came home late at night. There had been important assignments, as he would relate to us. We were extremely busy with typing for the resistance. For these reasons we got into the habit of going back to our rooms at night to do some more work. We always waited until Piet came home, and after Dina's "the coast is clear" signal, we would go downstairs.

FRIDAY NIGHT, JANUARY 21, 1944—A NIGHT OF INFAMY

On this night we were working in our room upstairs when the red light went on. It was about six o'clock. A small heater was on, and the table was filled with illegal papers, food coupons, names and addresses, as well as a heap of *Parool* newspapers.

Suddenly, we heard a terrific noise that consisted of yelling and screaming in German. It was the Gestapo, the dreaded German secret police. Felix, his face distorted in fear, motioned to me, then pointed toward the hiding cell. Gripped with panic and disbelief, we crawled into the place and—as the rehearsals had taught us—first locked the outside door and then the second inside door. There had been no time to hide any of the numerous papers on the table. The screaming downstairs was earsplitting. Even as we were sequestered in our hiding cell, we could hear the intruders giving commands. We could only guess what was going on.

My nightmare came true. We had come face-to-face with the enemy. Our lives and that of the Brandsen family were over. My heart pounded uncontrollably, and I began to feel the claustrophobia take over. I clung to Felix, desperately breathing for more air, my mind going as a windmill in the storm. What was to happen to Dina and the children? Where was Piet? How would the confrontation go when the Gestapo found us? I wanted to get out of there and unlock the doors. Felix held me back; I felt as if I had literally gone out of my mind.

Suddenly, we heard footsteps coming up the staircase. We knew exactly how many steps there were. As the person arrived at the top stair and reached for the doorknob, a voice yelled out in German, *"Was suchen Sie da, es gibt ja nichts da oben . . . "* Translated, this means, "What are you doing there, there is nothing upstairs." It must have been the head officer of the group, who wanted to show his superiority toward his subordinate; such was a characteristic of the "master race." We heard him go down the steps again, whereupon the yelling resumed. Clearly, the secret police were waiting for Piet.

As the fearful noise continued, we heard furniture being thrown, people stomping through rooms, Dina being ordered about. The minutes leaped into hours. What if the SS found the crystal radio or the secret papers? Where was Piet, and how were Dina and the children holding up?

Holding on to each other, Felix and I kissed each other good-bye, just as my sister had done when the German troops marched in; it seemed so long ago now. Felix began whispering the Kaddish, which is a prayer of mourning for the dead. In this prayer there are no complaints, only praise for God and for His wisdom. He also recited the Shema, the prayer of affirmation of our faith. It was all so surreal. My mind bounced back and forth from one terrifying thought to another as I gasped for air. My thinking was so distorted that at one minute I hoped that I would meet my mother in heaven, and the next I pictured Piet in danger, or dreamed how it would be to find freedom again.

Finally, finally, there was silence. We heard someone in our room then the voice of Dina calling out to us. After we crawled out of our cell, we looked at her face. Instantly we knew that a tragedy had occurred. Her face looked ashen, and tears were streaming down her cheeks. In between her sobs she said, "They have taken Piet; he had *Het Parool* paper in his pocket. They also arrested Piet Kerkhof, the neighbor's son, who came in to listen to the crystal radio. The Gestapo asked him what he was doing here, and he said he came over to borrow a book. They also took him to a concentration camp."

With a gesture of despair, she continued, "There were two SS officers, and one NSB. The NSB officer was the one who had climbed the stairs to your room, but was ordered to come back down."

Both Dina and I cried in desperation. Felix quickly picked up all of the papers from the table and put them in the hiding place. The three of us stood there in a tight embrace trying to absorb the tragedy that had taken place. Felix's face was stricken with sorrow. He said, "We cannot stay here any longer. They might come back to search the entire house."

Dina nodded, saying, "You cannot leave through the front door or the back door." She was right. The Germans had a habit of coming right back after a razzia or committing another crime. It was their way of slyly investigating other things that may have been going on against their ordinances.

Felix and I asked in a worried tone, "Where are the children? Are they all right?" Dina nodded. "I sent them to the neighbors." There was no more time to waste; we could stay no longer because our secret presence was a danger. Hugging us tightly, Dina uttered these last words to us, "I know a man who sometimes brought food to us. He knew that you were hidden here; they are good people and live in the outskirts somewhere, but it is far from here. His name is Hornsveld."

Our dear Piet had been betrayed for his work in the Resistance Movement. We wanted to ask Dina a thousand questions, but she had already left the room. We had to hurry—there was no time for anything anymore.

Chapter 30: The Vow

In a daze, we quickly put on our coats and went to the balcony off our room. It was icy cold and pitch dark outside. We stood on the balcony for a few minutes, not knowing what to do or where to go.

We knew that there was a gutter pipe on the left side of the balcony. Felix whispered to me to follow him as he climbed over the balcony railing and began sliding down the gutter. As if I were in a dream I followed him, and although I could hardly see a thing, I too went over the railing and slid down the gutter pipe.

Within a few minutes we stood on the ground. Taking a huge risk, we sneaked into the backyard and into the alley. Shivering from the bitter cold, Felix whispered, "We must reach the Van den Hoevens." We had met Mr. Van den Hoeven on a few occasions in the Brandsen's home, but we did not know where his house was. All we knew was that he lived on the same street as Piet and Dina.

One way or the other, we had to go back to the street. There were searchlights streaming from the sky as the Germans were scouring the air for Allied planes. For a moment, in my utter confusion, I had hoped for the bombings—perhaps, I thought, it would end this horrible nightmare I was living. Finally we reached the street, struggling through the slippery ground. A number of Dutch homes had entry doorways at that time. Each time a searchlight lit up the street, we hid in the doorway of a house, just like thieves. Felix whispered to me, "We can't go on like this. We have to ring a doorbell somewhere." We held on to each other, saying a silent prayer.

Taking a terrific chance, we rang the doorbell of the next house. A male voice called out, "Who is there?" Felix replied, with a quivering voice, "Piet Brandsen has been taken away by the Gestapo." Slowly the door opened, and yet another miracle occurred. It was Mr. Van den Hoeven. Our prayers had been heard. By the grace of God we had rung the right door-bell. Mr. Van den Hoeven said, "Come in quickly, before someone sees!"

With an alarmed expression on his face, Mr. Van den Hoeven asked us what had happened. After we told him that Piet had been arrested, his shock was even greater. He kept repeating, "Oh, my God, oh, my God." In the meantime, Mrs. Van den Hoeven had come to the hallway where we were standing. When she heard about the tragedy, she, too, became terrified; with her hands over her face, she kept lamenting and crying. Then an uncomfortable silence took over. Felix and I, in this desperate situation, could not say a word. We realized that our lives depended on what would take place within the next few minutes.

Finally, Mr. Van den Hoeven said, "We cannot have any more people in the house; as it is now, we already have five people here hiding." I was shaking uncontrollably, both from the cold and from my emotions. I said, "Dina mentioned the name of Hornsveld; he sometimes brought food, but we don't know where he lives."

Turning to his wife, Mr. Van den Hoeven nodded. "Yes, of course, I know where he lives. I was in his home a few times with Piet." First he looked at his wife, then at us. Then, as if he had suddenly come to a deci-sion, he said to us, "You know what? I will take you to the Hornsvelds. There is no other way." I saw that Mrs. Van den Hoeven's face turned from white to ashen. Although she did not object to her husband's pro-posal, she did admonish him by saying, "Please be careful; you know there is a curfew on."

It is difficult to describe our state of mind that night. We felt guilty for bringing others into danger; we feared for our lives. We felt as if we were a burden to people who, in essence, were total strangers. The anxiety we felt was overbearing.

As Mr. Van den Hoeven took a coat out of the hall closet, Mrs. Van den Hoeven motioned to us, saying, "Come upstairs with me; you have to say hello to your family. But please, make it short." We followed her up the steps and, as she opened a door, we saw our family members: Kurt, Nel, Felix's mother, and Kurt's mother. They were all lying on the bed. Needless to say, they were shocked to see us and to hear about the most recent tragedy. We quickly said hello and, just as quickly, good-bye. Felix's mother, who was holding a prayer book, put it down. She then placed her hands on our heads and recited a blessing in Hebrew. She cried softly.

Back in the downstairs hallway, Mr. Van den Hoeven said, "Well, let's go. I will walk ahead of you; the two of you must follow me. Be prepared that this is a dangerous undertaking." Before he opened the door, he took our hands and said, "Let's bow our heads and ask the Almighty for his blessing."

Mr. Van den Hoeven, an elderly man, had a difficult time walking against the raw, chilly wind. Now and then he waited for us, offering encouraging words. We passed by a number of canals, which we could faintly detect in the dark. After we had passed an ancient castle, we came to what looked like an empty terrain. Mr. Van den Hoeven seemed to know his way around; we continued to follow him through a narrow inlet. Finally, we approached a large house. "We are at the Hornsvelds' now," he said. "Thank goodness we did not encounter any Germans. I guess the Germans need their soldiers all over the globe."

The Hornsveld family

Mr. Van den Hoeven rang the bell. We heard footsteps then the voice of a woman. "Who is it?" she asked. "It is Van den Hoeven. I am here with a young couple. Piet Brandsen was arrested by the German police." The door opened slightly. Mr. Van den Hoeven stepped in, saying, "I have here a young Jewish couple. They need to stay overnight somewhere."

We stepped into the house, then the woman carefully locked the door. "This is Jan and Marietje," Mr. Van den Hoeven said. "They have nowhere to go. Please, could you have them over for one night?"

Poor Mr. Van den Hoeven had a difficult time catching his breath as he explained. Mrs. Hornsveld, a serious-looking, heavy-set woman of about forty, put her hand to her face and lamented, "Oh, how terrible! Oh, my God, what a tragedy! Poor Brandsen, and what about his wife and the four children?"

A shattering silence took over; I began, again, to shake from cold and fear. As I looked up to Mrs. Hornsveld, I thought she had grown somewhat; it must have been my imagination. She finally said, "My husband and my oldest son are not here right now, but I will ask my youngest son." She went to one of the rooms in the back of the hall, and we heard her say, "Bertus, come here. Piet Brandsen was arrested by the Germans."

A young man in his teens appeared. Mr. Van den Hoeven began to explain again what had happened. As I listened again, I wished for the ground to open up and swallow me right then and there. Then I heard Mrs. Hornsveld ask her son, "Can we have them for one night?" Bertus quickly answered, "Yes, we can!" Another miracle for Felix and me! We did not know it then, but his answer, "yes, we can," had determined our future forever.

Our next worry was Mr. Van den Hoeven's making his way back home safely. He said, "Thank God that this is solved for now. I have to get back right away." As he said good-bye, we gave him a big hug, wishing him Godspeed on his return trip. It was a staggering thought: Mr. Van den Hoeven walking that long distance alone in the dark, cold as ice, in the middle of a curfew. It was almost midnight by now.

After he left, Mrs. Hornsveld brought us into her front room and told us that her family knew all along that we were hiding at the Brandsen's home. On several occasions Mr. Hornsveld brought extra food to the Brandsen family, which Piet had shared with the Van den Hoevens. She explained that they, too, were helping with the "underground movement" by taking care of patriotic citizens whose husbands or sons had fallen prey to the Nazis. Both of her sons were involved.

Finally, she guided us upstairs to a room that had a window facing toward the back of the home. She said, "Listen carefully because what I am going to say is very important." She motioned toward the window and continued, "Here is the river, the Eem. Across from the river are the headquarters of the Gestapo. You must keep the curtains drawn. You must stay upstairs at all times because we have an office in our home downstairs with employees who must not know that you are here. My husband will explain everything to you tomorrow."

After that, she handed us some bed linens and blankets and wished us good night. She said, "We have to see tomorrow what my husband has to

A photograph of the back of the Hornsveld home and the open window of the room where we were hiding—which faced Gestapo headquarters

say." I remember saying to Felix, "What now?" He said again to me, "We are just in the hands of God."

I kept thinking, "I have abandoned God these past two years, and here we are, our prayers for help answered." Contemplating our uncertain future, I mentioned to Felix the subject of God. Fate meant for us to stay alive—so far. But on the other hand, I felt that my mother was gone forever. My thoughts went out again to all those who had been deported. What had become of them? Was God watching over them? What about our courageous Piet held in a concentration camp? We prayed intensely that night that his life would be spared.

Then Felix said with a determined tone in his voice, "It is now Friday night, January 21, 1944. The Shabbat has started. I am going to make a vow: I pledge to God that if we survive, I will do anything to keep the Jewish people together, wherever they might be in the world." His voice was trembling, and the emotion of that moment touched my heart deeply.

I asked God for forgiveness for my indifference over the past years. Holding hands, Felix and I prayed for courage to face the future. I remembered the words of the Hornsveld's young son. In later years, "Yes, we can," would become the opening phrase of my lectures about the Holocaust.

THE YEAR OF RENEWED HOPE

Chapter 31: Our New Travail

It was very early in the morning when we heard a knock on the door. It was Mrs. Hornsveld, who greeted us amicably and said, "You better come downstairs and have something to eat before the office help comes in." We followed her down the stairs to the large living room, where we had been the night before.

A lovely little girl was seated at the table. Mrs. Hornsveld said to us, "This is Corrie, our twelve-year-old daughter." Turning to Corrie she said, "This is Jan and Marietje. They stayed here overnight because Mr.

Corrie Hornsveld

Brandsen is in a concentration camp and they could not stay at the Brandsen home any longer."

Corrie simply smiled at us; we could see that she did not fully understand the situation. She was endowed with a beautiful color of blonde hair, a gorgeous complexion, and a captivating smile. A few minutes after our introduction to Corrie, her brother Bertus came into the room, greeting us with a cheery "good morning."

As we ate breakfast, I felt awkward. My self-esteem, which had dropped to such a minimal level because of all that had transpired, seemed to have completely vanished. Mrs. Hornsveld, noticing my sense of awkwardness and self-consciousness, pointed to me and said, "You must try to eat. You have to stay healthy and right now we have enough food."

She then began a conversation about the precarious situation in which we all were now involved. She told us that their oldest son, twenty-three-year-old Hannie, was hardly home and that he worked with a man named Koen, a friend of the family, who owned a commercial boat that transported freight. She also told us that her husband was expected home soon and hinted, with a gesture indicating secrecy, that he too was working for "The Cause."

Corrie, in her childish innocence, wanted to show us around the outside of the home, but Mrs. Hornsveld explained emphatically that from now on everyone in the house was to be very careful and discreet. She then took us to the office, which had a large window, to show us what the surroundings were like.

The house was very big and situated next to a large lumberyard, which Mr. Hornsveld managed. Behind the lumberyard was a body of water in which a number of small boats sat. Beyond was a meadow where cows and horses grazed. Beyond that was more water. The environment looked charming. It was, by all standards, a typical, peaceful Dutch landscape, worthy of a painting by one of Holland's great painters. It was snowing lightly outside, which added even more charm to the scene—it was breathtakingly beautiful.

We were on the outskirts of town and we realized, after seeing our surroundings, what a long walk it had been that terrible night from the

Van den Hoevens to the Hornsvelds'. We hoped that Mr. Van den Hoeven had made it back safely to his home.

Once again Mrs. Hornsveld spoke. "This area here is called De Grote Koppel aan de Eem." (Translated, this means, "The Big Belt on the River Eem." The name of Mr. Hornsveld's lumberyard was Houthandel Key, or "Lumberyard the Key.") Bertus then explained to us that a big building to the right of the lumberyard had been a crate factory, which the Germans had closed down. It was now used as a storage facility for hiding personal automobiles. Beyond were some neighbors and farther down, a tiny convenience store owned by a family named Bakker. The owner delivered his wares on a tricycle.

With the Gestapo headquarters across the river and the office personnel being unreliable, we were fully aware of the dangers of our hiding at the Hornsvelds. Even Bertus told us that he too was more or less confined to the indoors. Both boys held forged papers that identified them as shippers working for the Germans. Their friends in the underground created them, taking great care to exactly copy the German seal. The boys rarely left the house except at night to sabotage. And the supplies shipped up the river to the Germans were frequently minus a few cases by morning. In this way they could obtain food for their family and friends, but they were always, always on the alert for the dreaded Nazis. Bertus explained that the woodwork he was making kept him busy. It turned out later that he excelled in this craft.

By now it was time for us to go upstairs to our room and wait with much anxiety for Mr. Hornsveld. We felt extremely fearful for ourselves as well as for this family, who had suddenly found themselves with two strangers—not only a strange couple, but a Jewish couple, at a time when Jews were not supposed to be in existence in Holland any longer. We wondered how Mr. Hornsveld would react to us when he came home.

Felix and I realized that no one had ever been prepared to handle a situation like this—hiding people who were in danger and whose presence could bring grave peril. Felix, being a great analyst, said, "It will take a lot of patience, wisdom, and patriotism on both sides to overcome the many difficulties connected with hiding total strangers in one's home—and not even knowing for how long one will continue to do so."

We had heard from Piet that some people, on impulse and from the kindness of their hearts, had taken in persecuted people, not thinking of the reality of the danger. In some cases it did not work out, and the situations had ended in great tragedy. All these thoughts weighed heavily on our minds. Suddenly, a knock came at the door. A jolly-looking, rather portly man in his forties introduced himself as Henk Hornsveld. We shook hands and, as he seated himself on the bed, we began to talk. He said that he had known all along that we were hiding at the Brandsen's home and that he was also working for "The Cause" as a patriotic Dutch citizen. He expressed shock and regret over Piet's arrest by the Germans. We all talked of our worry about his fate and that of Dina and the children. For a while, the three of us were silent, in deep thought over our conversation.

Felix broke the silence by saying, "Mr. Hornsveld, we cannot begin to tell you how very concerned and sorry we are to put you and your family in such a dilemma, but we have nowhere to go." Mr. Hornsveld nodded sympathetically, although we detected some uncertainty in his facial expression; we fully understood his concern. For a few moments not a word was spoken—what could any of us say? But then, as Mr. Hornsveld was getting up from the bed, he said, "Let's try it out and see how it will work." This was the last we heard about this dilemma, either from Mr. Hornsveld or from Mrs. Hornsveld. As he was about to leave, he spoke these words, which I have never forgotten: "I don't expect less from myself than doing my utmost for my fellow man as a patriotic citizen."

Later that evening as we sat down for dinner with the family, the conversation again turned to the Brandsen family and to Piet in particular. Mr. Hornsveld said, "I will go to Dina and see if she needs help. You probably need your clothes and other things. I will pick them up for you."

I suddenly blurted out, "Oh, Mr. Hornsveld, all of our important documents and paper clippings are there! Our wedding papers and my mother's farewell letter and . . . " I began to stutter. "Everything in the metal boxes in Piet's backyard . . . " Now I began to cry bitterly. "Please ask Dina to save them." Mr. Hornsveld put his arms around me, assuring me that he would do his best. He said, "Just be calm." As an afterthought he said, "I am sure that Holland will be free again some day." Upon hearing the word "free," I again got a hold of myself and peace seemed to return to the dinner table.

The next morning something worrisome happened again. After breakfast, as Felix and I tiptoed through the hallway to go to our room upstairs, we ran into a person whom we had not seen before. It happened to be a salesman who worked for Mr. Hornsveld; he identified himself as Van Nus. We could tell by the look on his face that he figured out what was going on—the Hornsvelds were hiding a Jewish couple.

Mr. and Mrs. Hornsveld, who were in the hallway with us, looked quite concerned. Mr. Hornsveld began to explain in a calm tone that we were their guests from up north, but Van Nus, who was obviously a smart fellow, looked carefully at us and then at Mr. and Mrs. Hornsveld. As Mr. Hornsveld was telling a story, Van Nus interrupted him, winked, and said, "Ja, ja, ja." As Felix and I were standing forlornly in that hallway, Mrs. Hornsveld turned to Van Nus and with a no-nonsense tone said, "Look, this couple is here with us for now and I expect total discretion from you." Van Nus nodded, but he managed to ask, "What are their plans? Where are they going from here?"

Again, we were in the hands of a Higher Power. It was the worst question anyone could ask us during our odyssey through the Holocaust. Van Nus disappeared into the office, and we never saw him again. The incident was never brought up again.

Chapter 32: The Case
of the Air Raid Shelter

A few days later we met Hannie, the oldest son. He was a sturdy, buoyant-looking young man with a healthy, outdoors complexion. The office personnel had left, and we all sat down in the living room. Mr. and Mrs. Hornsveld began to explain what had happened and how Felix and I came to be there. Hannie nodded his head with an understanding expression on his face. All the while, he looked at us with a friendly smile.

There was a lot to discuss, and the parents wanted to point out to Hannie all of the dangers and problems associated with hiding us. There was a long list of things to consider: extra food coupons, the office staff, people coming in and out of the house, access to the air raid shelter. In short, things that were crucial to survival at that time could be thwarted by our presence.

After hearing about the risks, Hannie finally got up and said some very important words—words that lived with us for years, just as his brother's words had on the night we fled from the Brandsen's home. He said, "They must stay here; they are very welcome! I want only pros, no cons." Then everyone in the room shouted, "Pros only, no cons!" The experience of that afternoon is engraved in our hearts; it gave us a tremendous boost to know that the whole family was of one mind and spirit in hiding us from the horrid Nazis.

That evening Bertus asked his family, "What about Gerrie and Hisje?" Gerrie and Hisje were the girlfriends of the two sons who lived on a farm in a neighboring village and occasionally came to the Hornsveld's home to visit and bring food. We learned that because the girls came a great distance on their bikes—which at the time had wooden tires—they often stayed the night. Mrs. Hornsveld, looking at her sons, said, "Let's wait until they come and then decide what to do and how to do it."

Then Mr. Hornsveld asked to speak with us privately. He told us he had visited Dina Brandsen, and he assured us that she was doing the best she could under the circumstances. He told us that all of our paper clippings and documents were safe in the metal boxes hidden in the ground. We learned that the Van den Hoevens and Felix's family were doing all right. Mr. Hornsveld had also brought us some clothes for which we thanked him profusely.

One advantage of the Hornsveld's home was a second, small staircase leading from our room directly into the kitchen. Consequently, we did not have to be cooped up all day although we had to constantly be on the alert for strangers and the office staff. We had to be careful all of the time, as we had to use the same bathroom as the office staff. Watch out! was our motto. When the coast was clear, we would descend the stairs, sneak into the kitchen, and help Mrs. Hornsveld. We also took care of the family's dog, Kazan, to whom we became very attached.

The Hornsvelds also had a crystal radio in the attic. At nightfall we would go upstairs and listen to the BBC with the boys. It was the "Voice of the Free World," and we always hoped and prayed for good news.

We occasionally heard the voices of saboteurs on the radio, who spoke propaganda for the Germans. I vividly remember the British saboteur William Joyce, who became known as "Lord Haw Haw." There was also Iva d' Aquino, known as "Tokyo Rose," who broadcasted propaganda for Japan. After the war, a British court found "Lord Haw Haw" guilty of treason and he was hanged.

Since the house was located near a railroad station, much fighting went on during the daytime with sirens blasting constantly as fighter airplanes flew over us. The large air raid shelter was located in the field to the left of the house, and each time the alarm went off, the neighbors came running. Of course, we stayed indoors because no one was to know we were there. We would go to the cellar for protection, but my claustrophobia was so overwhelming that most of the time during the air raids I ran to the front entrance of the home and stood in panic near the door.

During our time there, we saw a lot of Corrie. She was a talented youngster and spent many hours drawing and sketching. She often came upstairs to our room always with a big smile on her face, ready to show off her work. We found that for such a young girl she was very talented. I predicted that some day she would be famous, and in later years this came true.

The family Hornsveld was wonderful to us; in just a short time they made us feel like family members. However, we had not yet met the sons' girlfriends. Felix and I had been with the Hornsvelds for two weeks, but the girlfriends had not ventured out to visit because it was dangerous to risk being out on ramshackle bicycles when bombings were going on during the day. Mr. Hornsveld, knowing the girls would finally visit within a short time, said to the boys, "We must tell the girls about Jan and Marietje; they have to know the truth. There are no two ways about it."

Finally, one afternoon Gerrie, Bertus' girlfriend, came to visit. Corrie called Felix and me to come down from our rooms to meet her. Gerrie was eighteen years old and very friendly looking. Her face glowed from the cold air and the long bike ride. When she first met us she looked surprised but did not ask any questions about us. She finally said, "Hisje will be here too." Mr. Hornsveld said, "Let's wait for Hisje; then we can explain everything."

We were all sitting in the living room when the doorbell rang. It was Hisje, a pretty girl of seventeen. She wore a colorful outfit with a lot of buttons running down the front. She joined us in the living room.

Mr. Hornsveld then told the girls who we were, the events that had taken place, and the circumstances that led to our hiding in their home. Gerrie, Bertus' girlfriend, took it all quite calmly. But Hisje became so nervous that she pulled most of the buttons off of her dress as she listened to the story.

Mrs. Hornsveld, a great diplomat and a gracious hostess, began to serve tea. With a fire roaring in the fireplace, the curtains drawn, and lights shining softly in the room we all talked. It became obvious that Hisje calmed down. At last, Mr. Hornsveld looked at Gerrie and Hisje and admonished, "Do not mention a word to your families. All of our lives depend on your secrecy." After the two young ladies gave their promise not to utter a word to anyone, they came over and gave Felix and me a hug. They exuded honesty and kindness. We liked them immediately and found them to be trustworthy young women.

Mr. Hornsveld continued talking, looking now at his sons. He said, "We need hiding places." The boys nodded. Hannie said, "You know what, we can utilize the space underneath the small staircase. We should start right away and take some measurements." Mr. Hornsveld and his sons had built boats and knew all about construction.

Suddenly we heard planes overhead, and the alarms began to sound. The ominous noise of the sirens along with the tumultuous roar of the approaching planes caused everyone to run to the air raid shelter. The noise was earsplitting. Felix pulled me by the arm and we ran to the cellar. The bombing and fighting going on over our heads seemed endless. I could not stand it any longer, and I ran out of the cellar into the hallway and toward the front entrance near the door. Suddenly there was a loud and heavy thud—similar to the sound of a thunderbolt. I was convinced that something had crashed right on the house. Felix came running down the hall. He wanted me to come back into the cellar, but I was so frightened I was sure I would suffocate down there. After what seemed like hours, the "all clear" signal sounded and the family came out of the shelter.

Large pieces of metal from an airplane had plunged right in front of the door from which I was standing just a few feet away. If these pieces had landed any closer I would have been dead. Felix and I and the family stood there, looking at the large pieces of metal for a long time; all of us were in shock. The men were trying to figure out whether the pieces were from an Allied plane or a German plane that had crashed; they were anxious to know where it had come down.

Mrs. Hornsveld finally came forward, and with a stern expression on her face said, "This is it. From now on I want Jan and Marietje in the shelter also. If something bad happens we don't want that on our conscience." Everyone agreed. Mr. Hornsveld added, "Absolutely, Ma is right. We'll think of something to explain to the neighbors. I'll work something out."

The next day the girls left for home. We said good-bye and wished them well on their way back. In our room upstairs later that day, Felix and I thought deeply about the events of that weekend. We were both impressed that the girls showed great understanding, sympathy, and dignity in the face of such danger.

Our loved ones were never out of our thoughts: Piet, Dina, my mother, and all of the rest of our family. But we were grateful that once more, we had been guided by a Higher Force and had met wonderful people along our frightful journey through the Holocaust.

Chapter 33: The Uniform

In a relatively short time, Mr. Hornsveld and his sons had constructed several hiding places. Since the house was very large and old, it was easy to find spaces for hiding. There were many nooks and crannies that were suitable for this purpose.

We now had one hiding place upstairs that was easy to approach from our room in case something suspicious went on downstairs. Underneath the small staircase near the kitchen was a large, secret space which was later used as sleeping quarters for Hannie. One had to crawl in this small space and place a wood barrier over the opening. There was also a huge place to hide in the attic. Two people could easily hide and sleep in there. In the event of danger, a hatch closed from the inside, a rug was thrown over it, and no one would suspect that people could be in there.

Mr. and Mrs. Hornsveld suggested that we call them aunt and uncle and so they became "Tante Cor and Oom Henk" (Aunt Cor and Uncle Henk). It came easily to us, because we had become quite attached to the family. We did not know how to express our gratitude for all they did for us; we tried to make ourselves as useful as possible. I especially tried to be useful in the kitchen; after all, I was the "niece."

We learned from the BBC, via the crystal radio, how the war was escalating. Hundreds, perhaps thousands, of Allied planes buzzed over our roof every night, always at the same time. We heard about the terrific bombing of strategic points in Germany. I was always both fearful and happy to hear them fly over our heads: fearful that they would be shot down; happy to know they were bombing the barbaric enemy.

In late February 1944, the Allied Air Forces blasted industrial targets in Germany, such as railroads and factories. We heard through the crystal radio that these bombings would change the history of the war. Aircraft plants and many important factories in the major cities in Germany were destroyed. The Germans became frantic to such an extent that they began to pick up anybody from the streets. On orders from Seyss-Inquart, people had to be deported to work for the war machine. No one was safe any longer. The Germans used the same tactics on others that they had used on the Jewish population.

We knew that Uncle Henk was deeply involved with the resistance, but contrary to Piet's openness, Oom Henk was very secretive about it. The only thing he had mentioned to us was that the newspaper, *Het Parool,* had continued to be printed and circulated in Amersfoort. No suspicion about this could fall on Piet. But none of us knew where Piet was or how he was doing. It was an awful feeling.

One evening at dinner Uncle Henk in a quiet tone said, "Before another huge bombardment comes along and we have to go into the shelter with the neighbors, I must tell you that I confided to some friends that you two are hiding in our home." I must have turned pale because he continued, "Marietje, calm yourself. I have some positive news to go along with this." We held our breath as we waited for his next words. He said, "I have a uniform for Jan. It is a clever idea because the uniform can function as a postman's, as well as a German soldier's. Let me show you what it looks like."

Uncle Henk then left the room and shortly returned with a package. Out came a uniform. He said, "Come on, Jan, let's go upstairs and see if it fits you." Felix and I were stunned into silence, but Felix followed Uncle Henk. Bertus said, "That's Pa! He doesn't mince words."

After a short while the door opened and there was Felix in a German officer's uniform. He could truly have posed for a German; it was so strange to me! Uncle Henk remarked, "You know, whoever made this was very, very smart, because it fits Jan to a tee." He then reached into the package and out came a number of accessories that were interchangeable. It was incredible! Inside the air raid shelter, Felix could be a postman. If necessary, the outfit could also be viewed as a German uniform. It turned out that later on, it would be a lifesaver in a serious situation in which we found ourselves.

The weather was still bitter cold. There was a thin layer of ice on the river. With the approval of Uncle Henk and Aunt Cor, we'd open the front door at night to get some fresh air; we had been confined to the indoors for so long that we needed to get away from our room upstairs now and then. We frequently did exercises and deep breathing during these nights with Corrie on the lookout for strangers!

One evening, as we were standing outside, we suddenly heard a man screaming loudly for help in German. A drunk German officer had fallen into the river. When we saw the neighbors come running down toward the river because of the commotion, Felix and I dashed upstairs. Koen and Hannie had been working on the boat, which was moored to the back of the house. We lifted the curtains just a little to see what was happening.

We then saw Hannie—who was always eager to help—jump into the water to try to save the man. All the while we heard neighbors shouting obscenities, yelling for Hannie to throw the German back into the canal. While Koen and Hannie hoisted the German onto the boat, the soldier kept jabbering about his cap that was in the water. We later learned that in the German army it is a big offense to lose one's cap.

Against all logic, Hannie brought the man into the house to a room downstairs. The man, shivering badly, stammered, "Heiss, heiss," meaning "hot, hot." There was not even a heater on! Hannie quickly gave him some dry clothes and ordered a cab for him. It turned out that the man was a sergeant stationed at the Dumolin barracks in Amersfoort. The next day the German came back to the house with a coupon for Hannie to purchase shoes as replacement for the shoes that had ended up in the river.

It is not difficult to imagine the impression this event had on all of us. Should Hannie have let him drown? Had he done the right thing to save the enemy? Had he compromised, or was saving the German the only option? This was the topic of discussion many times. Hannie had saved one life, but the enemy had taken millions. We wondered also how the neighbors had felt about this.

After many discussions, Uncle Henk said, "Look, if a similar situation happens again, we must simply stay out of it. Many people drown in the canals at night when it is dark. We must not continue to dwell on this." Turning to Hannie, Henk said, "I want to remind you that we have two people hiding here, so think about that in the future."

There are many facets of ethics in life. Several weeks later, another German, an SS officer from the secret police, fell into the river and drowned. There had been no one around to save him. In revenge, the Gestapo lined up seven innocent civilians and executed them on the spot in view of people who were ordered to watch. Such was the barbaric act of the German "master race."

Shortly after this incident, we had to go into the shelter. The bombings were now continuous. We could see planes burning in the air, plunging to the ground not far from the house. War tears on one's heart in a dreadful way.

The first time that Felix went into the shelter with his uniform, someone asked, "Where are you from and who are you?" Before he could answer, the tumult of the bombings drowned out all other sound; it was terrifying. Some of the neighbors were praying; all of us were panic-stricken, hoping to survive. When the bombings stopped, not one of the neighbors asked Felix any further questions. All of us were aware that the Allies were helping us and that eventually the liberation would come.

Chapter 34: D Day and Missiles

Since we could not work for *Het Parool* any longer, the days upstairs became excruciatingly long. Felix still kept his diary, but that did not take up much time. We hid the notes to the diary in the hiding place near our room.

One day, Felix asked Uncle Henk if there was anything he could do that would occupy his time. Perhaps there was something special he could think of. Uncle Henk understood fully how slow the days were going by for Felix. Henk said, "Let me think about it; maybe I might know of something." I kept myself useful by helping Aunt Cor in the kitchen, or doing sewing work, or other household chores. For me, the days went by much faster.

A few days later Uncle Henk came to us with a triumphant look on his face. He said, "Jan, by golly I have found something for you to do. Come to the attic and I'll show you what it is. I went up with them because I was curious as to what it could possibly be. When we got to the attic, there it was! We saw lots of colorful tiles and a heap of cement on the floor. Uncle Henk said, "I will show you and explain what can be done with all of that. The days will fly by for you!" He then showed Felix how to work the cement and the tiles so that one could make colorful flowerpots out of them. I was so happy that Felix was able to do something so useful.

From then on, Felix spent days on end in the attic. In time, he became an expert at making flower pots, ashtrays, and many items that were useful for a household. In fact, he became so experienced and innovative with this hobby that Uncle Henk saw fit to sell the items or exchange them for food. Even the air raids could not deter Felix from leaving the attic at times.

Despite the fact that this work gave both of us some peace of mind, everyone in the household had to be constantly on guard, and each of us was always edgy, not knowing what the sadistic Germans had in mind.

But luckily, one day we heard on the crystal radio that the Russians, who had recaptured Kiev at the end of 1943, had now broken the siege of Leningrad. When Felix predicted with certainty that Germany would lose the war, I began to feel somewhat less lethargic, and I began to daydream of freedom and how it would feel for life to be normal again.

Then, on Tuesday, June 6, 1944, we heard the exciting news that made us realize that the course of the war—and our lives—would change. It was a day never to be forgotten.

The men had gone upstairs to listen to the crystal radio while Aunt Cor and I were downstairs repairing some clothes. Corrie was drawing and making sketches. Suddenly, Felix came running downstairs and with full speed ran into the room we were in, his eyes open wide with excitement, his face glowing. "Come quick, hurry up!" Felix shouted. "The Allies have landed in Normandy!" We threw our sewing to the floor and in a frenzy ran upstairs. And there we heard it: the announcer from England broke the news, "THE ALLIES HAVE LANDED IN NORMANDY!"

These words were repeated over and over again. Even though there was a lot of static and creaking on the little radio, we continued to listen and savor the words, not wanting to lose one syllable from this incredible news. Everything, it seemed, took on a new meaning, leaving us with renewed hope.

However, just as we were basking in the hope for freedom, something again happened. About a week after the good news of the Allies landing in Normandy, while we were sitting at dinner we heard an ominous roar outside. We had never heard such an eerie sound before. All of us flew out of the room in different directions. I landed in the W.C., which had a small window out of which I could look outside. We saw a huge object with a great flame on its tail roaring over our area; the sound was unearthly. Then the sound stopped suddenly and we heard an enormous explosion nearby. It instantly reminded me of the explosion on the SS *Simon Bolivar*. There had been no air raid warning. Just the same, everyone ran into the air raid shelter, even Felix without his uniform.

We did not know what it was and where it came from; for certain, it was not an airplane. Just as we were about to leave the shelter, a second object roared by with tremendous speed. That, too, exploded near our area. The neighbors started to talk with each other and one of them began to curse. "Damn," he shouted. "When will that cursed war ever end!" Then, another person came forward and said, "It must be a rocket . . . we must find out where it exploded."

But the next day we learned that the Germans had indeed fired missiles; they were called V-1s. This news was all in the papers. The Germans were quite proud of their attacks. Now, the horror of the missiles continued on a daily basis. We soon learned that when the sound stopped, the missile would soon explode. It would then hit the civilian population, which suffered great losses of lives.

The joyous expectations for freedom were gone for the time being. Every day I spent hours of agony in the bathroom, listening and waiting for missiles. Later on, the Germans developed even stronger missiles. They were called V-2s. They were much bigger, like flying monsters that roared with huge flames through the air.

Uncle Henk learned that the missiles were fired not far off from where we lived and that V-2s could travel faster than the speed of sound. It was awesome, because we could not hear them coming—they zoomed by in a second. Through the BBC, we learned that the missiles could reach a height of sixty miles and then suddenly dive toward their target.

At night, I constantly stayed awake listening for those dreaded missiles. Added to this was the sound of the Allied planes flying over our heads by the hundreds. It was a nightmare. One night in desperation, I said to Felix, "I can't stand it any longer. Bring me poison!" Felix became upset with me, saying, "Don't give up now; get a hold of yourself. The end of the war is near and you have to grit your teeth." I tried hard not to show my fear to the Hornsvelds; yet again, I lost weight because I could not eat or sleep.

We learned from the BBC that the missiles had reached London for the first time in June 1944, causing tremendous damage. We all felt great compassion for the brave people of England, and we greatly admired their perseverance, despite the unimaginable air attacks they suffered.

Meanwhile we held fast to the news. We learned that the United States forces had broken out of Normandy and that Romania and Bulgaria had declared war on Germany. That little radio was truly our salvation, and it gave me a reason to pull myself together.

I spent the nights alone in our room because the family wanted Felix and the boys hidden; they feared the boys would be forced to serve in the German army if found. Felix and Bertus slept together in the large space in the ceiling. Hannie, who was home now, slept in the hiding place underneath the stairway on the first floor.

We could tell from the actions of the Germans and also from the information in the newspapers that the enemy had become reckless. They were indifferent to the suffering of the population and indiscriminate in shooting off their rockets. Food became very scarce—almost unobtainable.

All of us had reached a low point not knowing how long this infernal war would last. But on July 18, 1944, some very good news reached us. We heard on the BBC that the U.S. Army, led by General Omar Bradley, had broken out of Normandy's peninsula and was sweeping across France. It was exciting news.

Then, on the evening of July 20, 1944, the most unbelievable news of all was reported on the radio. A German by the name of Colonel Count von Stauffenberg had tried to assassinate Hitler. He had placed a time bomb under Hitler's table during a staff meeting. Unfortunately, Hitler had only been slightly wounded. We had hoped that this would be the end of the war. Von Stauffenberg, after being brutally tortured by his own people, was executed.

Immediately following all of these highly emotional events, Felix became quite ill. He developed a high fever; his lips, eyes, and entire face swelled up so badly that he looked grotesque. All of the pressures, tensions, and anxieties seemed to have come to a head. It was clear that a doctor had to be called.

Chapter 35: Mad Tuesday

A doctor came to the house to check on Felix that evening. The family had assured us that Dr. Plomp was a good, patriotic person. He seemed friendly and relaxed as he shook hands with us. I was present as the Hornsvelds explained to the doctor who we were and how we got there.

I followed the doctor upstairs. After he examined Felix thoroughly, he turned to me and said, "Your husband has urticaria; it is an allergic reaction." He indicated to Felix that he would be back in a few days and then said to me, "I will talk to you downstairs." Upon reaching the large hallway, Dr. Plomp said to me, "Your husband is very sick. He needs complete rest and special food. He is young and will make it, but he needs care. As much as possible, keep him away from worrisome news."

The doctor also spoke with the Hornsvelds. It gave me a good feeling to know that he would be back again to check on Felix. As he was leaving, he said to me in Dutch (loosely translated), "Hold on tight, freedom is around the corner!"

To become so ill while in hiding and to be so dependent upon strangers was very difficult to say the least. But somehow we had been blessed with encountering with such good people along the way, people who had shown compassion and love for their fellow citizens.

When I came downstairs the next morning for breakfast, I asked, "Where is Uncle Henk?" The family told me that he had left very early that morning for nearby farms to secure special food for Felix. I was truly moved, almost to tears.

Up until now, there had been adequate food for all of us at the Hornsveld's home. However, eggs, milk, and meat were almost unattainable. A number of people had begun to eat cats, which were called "roof rabbits." Many became despondent over the lack of certain types of food.

The Germans did not care a bit about the civilians; they kept the best and the most abundant foods for themselves. Many people began to die of starvation, and tuberculosis became rampant.

Uncle Henk knew how to get food—he worked secretly with the resistance. The underground movement in Holland had its own methods of stealing food from the Germans, which, of course, had been stolen from the Dutch people to begin with. The Dutch, being quite shrewd, had their ways to fool the Germans on many occasions. But as we learned later, many had lost their lives along the way. Acquiring potatoes was considered a heroic act!

With the extra food that Uncle Henk brought home and the fact that Felix was young, he was soon on the road to recovery. Dr. Plomp paid another visit to check on Felix and assured us that his illness would not leave any lasting scars. The swelling on his face and body began to slowly disappear.

SEPTEMBER 5, 1944—MAD TUESDAY

September 5, 1944, went down in Dutch history as *Dolle Dinsdag,* meaning "Mad Tuesday." On this day, the Allied troops advanced with great speed through northern France and Belgium. This news spread quickly. Parts of the south of Holland had been liberated, and the citizens up north were convinced that the Allied troops would also reach the northern cities the same day!

But the Allied troops had to wait for more supplies in order to be able to push up to the north. This fast-spreading news, combined with the intoxicating feeling of impending liberation among the Dutch, caused the people to lose a sense of reality. Five years of horror, crimes, and persecutions would now come to an end, or so they thought. Dutch flags were raised all over; people went out into the streets screaming, "They are here! They are here! Our liberators are here!" That was a day of mass hysteria.

The hours went by and no Allied troops were seen in the north. Dreams of a fast liberation went up in smoke. We did not know it then, but we still had to make it through the winter, and the winter of 1944 was to be the worst ever. The Germans resumed their unspeakable atrocities toward the Dutch people by shooting everyone who had Dutch flags raised or who they had suspected were opposed to them. The Germans did not have to answer to anyone, so they shot anyone at random! Premature enthusiasm turned into deadly horror as the worst winter of the war loomed ahead of us.

We had to be extra careful from then on, especially since we had spotted Germans in our area. Then, on September 15, 1944, another unbelievable event took place. It was very early in the morning that we heard the sound of what we had thought were thousands of Allied airplanes flying overhead. We all ran upstairs to the attic, which had a large window. Looking out, we saw hundreds of paratroopers coming down not far from our home. We became absolutely crazy with excitement. We cried and yelled to each other, "This is it! This is real! They are coming!"

Hannie quickly went to get the hidden crystal radio. All of us wanted to listen, but we did not want to keep our eyes off of the paratroopers. We learned from the BBC that this was the largest airborne operation ever, dropping three divisions from almost five thousand planes and sliders onto the town of Arnhem to seize bridges in advance of the ground forces. We heard later that, unfortunately, only part of the Allied objectives had been successful. Thousands of men were killed on both sides. All of us took this news very badly, and our hearts went out to the courageous soldiers of the Allied forces. Many years later, a movie was made about this event called "A Bridge Too Far."

We knew from the BBC that the First Army had crossed the German border in mid-September, and that General Eisenhower had planned to knock out the dreaded V-2 launching sites in Holland.

There was no end to our many conversations. Will the war end soon? we wondered. How much longer will we have the Rot-Moffen on our land? How many more victims will die? Our worries went on and on. By now, the Dutch people were convinced that the liberation was near. Some people talked about the "German Capitulation." However, the resistance papers warned everyone not to be too optimistic and to wait until the Canadians were here. But we heard through the resistance that many in the NSB had fled Holland already. They anticipated their fate when Holland would finally be free.

We wondered about the German occupation forces in Holland. Did they know all that was going on? Would they know that France was free? What about Belgium and the south of Holland? It seemed that they were unaware because their behavior continued just as sadistically as before.

Nevertheless, all of us were swept away with the thought of freedom. Corrie and I began to get outdoors at night, and we often walked through the meadow enjoying the fresh air. The fighting over our heads went on, and the air raids happened sometimes when we were a distance away from the house. During those times we had to run quickly to the shelter for safety.

There was always a lot of gossip among neighbors when we were in the shelter. One time we overheard someone state that the British dropped weapons off at certain Dutch points to be used when the Allied troops would come. Hannie kept us up-to-date on what went on in Holland because he heard the local news from Koen, who still used his boat to load freight.

Then one day, in the beginning of October, the best news of all came to us: Piet Brandsen was home! At last, our fervent prayers were answered!

Chapter 36: The Visit

It happened when I was working in the kitchen. Aunt Cor ran in; her face was flushed and she was very excited. "Marietje," she uttered in an almost breathless manner, "There is a great surprise, and here it is!" She motioned to someone in the hallway and in came Piet Brandsen.

I let out a big yell, and as I flew into his arms I had to gasp for breath. I could not speak; the emotion was overwhelming. I heard Aunt Cor going up the stairs to get Felix. He came down immediately, and when he saw Piet, he too was overwhelmed. At first, like me, Felix was so stunned he was speechless. Piet looked sickly. He had little color in his face, and he had lost much weight. We could only surmise how he must have suffered at the hands of the Nazis.

We all sat down in the big room and, finally, out came a flood of questions from Felix and me. We had to know everything. Piet told us that he had been released from the camp just a few days before. The Nazis had interrogated him for months; Piet, however, never lost control and stuck to his original story. He told them he had found a copy of *Het Parool* on the train. He denied having anything to do with the resistance. He kept his nerves under control at all times and never once changed his story. We asked him about Piet Kerkhof, the young son of the neighbors of Piet and Dina, whom the Gestapo had arrested at the same time. Piet told us that the Nazis had dismissed him after four months in the camp.

It is difficult to describe our happiness upon Piet's return, especially knowing that it was not Felix and I who had precipitated his arrest. Piet told us that Dina and the children had been brave throughout the ordeal. He did not want to discuss the gory details of his time in the camp; in fact, he never disclosed any of these details to anyone after his release.

We spent a long time together that morning. When Aunt Cor left the room, Piet, quite emotionally, said to us, "I want to ask the two of you to come back to us and stay until the end of the war. We have gone through thick and thin together, and I don't want to give up now that the end is in sight." We were moved to tears, especially when he added, "Dina and the children want you back, too."

Felix and I were speechless and deeply touched. My tears began to flow. Piet took our hands in his and said, "Look, think about it. Both Dina and I would like for you to come back. If you want to stay here, then I expect you to come and stay at least a few days with us."

When Piet left, Felix and I went to our room. We did not speak for a long time, and when we finally broke our silence we were filled with emotion. I said, "I hope Piet will gain back his weight; he is not the same Piet anymore." "That will be impossible," Felix replied. "Without good food it will be very difficult." But we knew that his friends from the resistance would think of a way to secretly provide food for him.

Although we had gained some peace of mind upon Piet's return, none of us were able to relax. The dreaded V-2 missiles that were launched from sites in our country continued without mercy. We had heard on the radio that the city of Antwerp had suffered terrible losses from the rockets, and thousands of people were dead or seriously injured.

Our queen spoke often to the nation, trying to instill hope and pleading for patience. She always poured her heart into her speeches, urging the citizens to "hang in there." She ended each speech with the words, "May God be with you. Holland shall be free!"

The family kept the crystal radio on all of the time. The men took turns listening, and we talked endlessly about the war. We closely followed the news about the United States forces and the Canadian troops, which were making great advances all over. But we realized that we, who lived in the north, had a long wait before the end.

Uncle Henk had a sister who lived with her family on the other side of town. They were nice people who visited often; on occasion, they spent the night. Uncle Henk's sister's name was Rika, and her husband's name was Henk. They had two children: a teenage daughter named Greta and a ten-year-old boy named Henkie. Of course, there had been no choice but for Uncle Henk and Aunt Cor to tell them who we were, so we also called them aunt and uncle. Later, they would play a life-saving role in our lives during the last stages of the war. Piet visited us often, and we could see that it bothered him not to have us in his home. He insisted that we should come for a day. Even when we told him it would be risky for us to leave, he assured us that the Germans were too busy with the way the war was going. Piet had an overpowering personality. He had done much for us; in fact, he had saved our lives and those of Felix's family. I suppose we were drawn under his spell, and finally we could no longer refuse his persuasive requests.

We discussed everything openly with the Hornsvelds. Obviously, they were very surprised, especially since Piet had just been released from a concentration camp. Felix and I did not know what to do. The Hornsvelds pointed out the many dangers in the area. Deep in our own hearts we understood that for Piet, this was a matter of honor, combined with genuine love and friendship for us.

Somehow we lacked the courage to refuse Piet's request. We felt obligated to him for having saved our lives at the darkest and most dangerous period of the persecutions. Finally, after weighing the risks, we gained the reluctant approval of the Hornvelds, and Piet was notified of our upcoming visit.

And so, on a Sunday at six o'clock in the morning we began our trek to the Brandsen's home. We left early in the hope of avoiding an encounter with anyone. I remember how incredibly cold it was. Our "false" identity papers were safely tucked in our pockets. Felix wore his uniform with the postal insignias attached. I was quite nervous, and I remember how I constantly looked behind me to see if anyone was following us. Felix, however, did not display any fear.

A worrisome part of our trip was the small inlet leading to the town because there were a number of houses that we had to pass. Several people who had met us in the air raid shelter lived in these homes, and they must have had an inkling of who we were and where we stayed. We walked calmly, acting as if this was our daily exercise. Felix and I had carefully discussed the various possibilities that could take place as we made our way to the Brandsens'. For instance, we decided that if an air raid took place, we would not go into anyone's home. And if a German stopped us, Felix would speak in German and react carefully, according to the situation.

Once we made it through the inlet, all went well. We had not met any German soldiers. Finally, we came to Piet's street, and after entering the notorious alley, I let out a sigh of relief; at last, the first part of this mad undertaking was over. But as Felix and I walked through Piet's backyard, the memories of the night of terror, when Piet was arrested by the Gestapo, began to haunt me, and I began to doubt the wisdom of our visit.

The family Brandsen was waiting for us. What a reunion it was! The children were adorable; they did not want to let go of us; they clung so fast. There was so much to talk about. We asked about Opa, the neighbors, and how Piet Kerkhoff had fared in that horrible concentration camp. We talked about the family Van den Hoeven, about Felix's family, and how Kurt's mother was holding up, especially with her diabetes. For hours we discussed the course of the war and the food rations.

Piet and Dina

Piet had arranged with the Van den Hoevens for Kurt to come to the Brandsen home around dusk. The Van den Hoeven family was very reluctant for us to come to their home, which we understood quite well.

Aside from the air raids, for which we did not run into the shelter, the day went by too quickly and too pleasantly. But as dusk began to set in, I became edgy and hoped that Kurt would come quickly. Indeed, within minutes after dusk he entered through the kitchen. As we embraced he said, "Our mothers are holding up well. Nel is okay, but the food is a big problem. We will manage the best we can," he added with a worrisome look on his face.

It seemed to me that the conversation went on endlessly, and I began to remind everyone that we had to leave and make our way back. The Brandsens wanted us to spend the night, but we politely declined—we knew the Hornsvelds would worry. We had to be back before curfew.

As Kurt left, Felix and I also parted with many hugs and kisses. Dina and the children made the sign of the cross as we left and wished us Godspeed along our way. Walking from the alley to the street, I once again became overwhelmed with that ominous feeling of fear. As we walked through the streets, I became haunted by past experiences, and the tension in my body rose. In my imagination, I saw the Gestapo coming after us. Darkness had set in. It was difficult to see where we were going. But we recognized the canals and just as we detected the vague outlines of the ancient castle that we had to pass that led to the inlet, my ominous feelings turned into reality.

Before me was my nightmare: a German sentry was standing guard. He approached us and, shining his flashlight on us, yelled "Halt!" As he came nearer, he shouted in German, "Who are you? Where are you going?" My heart began to pound, and my body began to shake. The soldier looked suspiciously at Felix's uniform, and I saw by the expression on his face that he wondered what profession Felix was in.

Thank goodness Felix was well prepared. The soldier's uniform did not have the dreaded Gestapo or SS insignias on it, and Felix began to speak to him in German, his native tongue. In a brusque tone of voice, Felix said with unbelievable confidence, "What do you mean? We live right here on a boat; we are out on our evening walk." The German looked around a bit, but I believe, on account of the dark, he could not see much. Only Koen's boat was there.

Then Felix said sternly, "Look, we have to get through and if you don't let us in, I will report it to your superior." The man must have been mightily impressed with Felix, and upon hearing the word "superior," he let us go. Of all things, he clicked his heels, saluted, and disappeared into the dark.

It was an unforgettable experience. When we were safely back with the Hornsvelds we told them our story. It taught all of us a lesson not to act prematurely. The war was still raging on and all of us had a long, long way to go.

THE ROAD TO FREEDOM

Chapter 37: The Tunnel

One evening, when the family Brandt was visiting, Hannie stormed into the room. Looking at his father, he shouted in an excited voice, "Pa, guess what happened! The Germans have stolen all the cars out of the crate factory, and they have filled it up with grain. The whole building is overflowing with grain." We were stunned by this news. The cars belonged to private citizens who had hid them in the empty factory, thinking that the vehicles would be safe there.

Pa asked, "How do you know?" "From Koen," Hannie continued, swallowing hard from excitement. "He saw the whole thing. The Moffen have stolen everything from the farmers and we must do something about it." Turning to Bertus he pleaded, "Bert, you have to help and we must do something before the Moffen take the grain to Germany. It is a must."

Pa, as always, did not react at first; he was deep in thought. We all knew we had come to the point where the surrogate food was inedible. The farmers also were at their last resources with most of their livestock gone. Finally after a long silence, Pa said, "However do you think that we can pull anything off without being caught?" Hannie, with great confidence and youthful vigor, replied, "I will think of something. We must come up with a plan; we must fool the Moffen ."

Uncle Henk's office staff was gone, and we had more freedom now. Instead of addressing our hosts as "aunt" and "uncle," we found it was easier and shorter to call them "Moe" and "Pa."

The following days were spent talking about the "plan." Hannie, the happy-go-lucky young man, constantly thinking of new ideas, never saw any danger in anything. Bertus had his father's character—always carefully planning things out into minute detail and never acting in haste. A few days later, Hannie announced that he had a great idea. He spoke with much enthusiasm. "Listen, I have it all worked out," he said. "We must dig a tunnel and then get to the inside of the factory and get to the grain." No one said a word at first. But then Bertus spoke. "I think we can pull it off," he said, "if we do it during the night."

I could see that Pa was hesitant. Finally after much discourse, the decision was made, mostly because of the scarcity of food and the prospect of a long winter ahead. And thus, with the okay from Pa, the boys prepared themselves for this daring adventure.

The next evening, assisted by their Uncle Henk Brandt, they began to work on digging a tunnel. Each night, when they returned home safely, we sighed in relief. After a week had gone by, they triumphantly announced that the tunnel was ready. They had found a way to connect the tunnel to the factory, and they were set to go!

Now we had to work on all of the details of who should go through, what time of night, how to get the grain out, and who should be on the lookout for Germans. It was decided that Corrie should stand guard. Each night we talked and talked, until all of us were completely swept up in the enthusiasm. Felix and I immediately volunteered to come along with the Hornsveld family into the tunnel. The family Brandt would also join in. Koen had given Hannie a large supply of cloth sacks; in turn, Hannie promised to give him part of the grain. Koen had added, "I hope you will be successful; I'll keep an eye out for you." Uncle Henk, now quite emotionally involved in the plan, said jokingly, "What the heck, let's take as much as we can from the Rot-Moffen."

The next night, when it was very late, all of us sneaked out toward the tunnel with a cloth sack in our hands. It was pitch dark and very cold, but we could not wear heavy clothes; we needed to fit in the narrow tunnel. We crawled in and when the last of us had reached the inside, we fell down in the middle of the grain. The tension had been awesome. We could not see a thing; we could only feel the grain around us. It was so dusty that Aunt

Rika began to sneeze incessantly. Her husband had to hold his hand over her face the whole time. After a short rest, we began to fill up the sacks, using our hands. It took a very long time.

Each time that we thought we heard something, we hid under the grain. It must have been mice running around. It seemed like an eternity before our mission was over; we were in there for a long time, always listening for possible dangers. Finally, after hours had gone by and we had filled the sacks, we had to crawl out of the tunnel, toting the very heavy sacks behind us. Going into the tunnel with empty sacks was nothing compared to our journey back with the very heavy loads. By then it was three o'clock in the morning. We found little Corrie bravely standing guard. We reached the house safely, worn out, excited, tired, but happy. There was now enough food to last for a while. Of course we shared our grain with the Van den Hoevens, and Koen got his share, as well. It had been another daring adventure that had ended safely.

Perhaps because we were not used to eating the heavy grain, or perhaps because of the excitement, Felix and I became quite sick with dysentery. We both had high fevers, but we refused to have a doctor come to the house. Aunt Cor, who was quite concerned, had us use several old Dutch folk remedies, which seemed to help because slowly we began to recuperate, although the illness left us weak for a long time.

That particular winter of 1944 was the worst that I can remember. Knowing that part of southern Holland was free, our hopes had been raised for liberation. It was not yet to be. In December the Allies—before they could cross the Rhine River—had to face a last-stand German onslaught in the Ardennes Forest. It had come as a complete surprise for the Allies. The "Battle of the Bulge," as it was called, had begun.

We listened day and night to the BBC. Felix, meanwhile, wrote feverishly in his diary—it was now many, many pages, all written in pencil. I often said, "How senseless is war; everyone loses; all those young lives are snuffed out because of the Germans and their crazy Führer." I asked why this horrible fight was called "The Battle of the Bulge," and Felix explained that the bulging shape of the battleground could be seen on the map. As a matter of fact, the Hornsvelds, Felix, and I looked at an old atlas, and in our minds, we followed the Allied troops, trying to figure out where they were, how the war progressed, and when it would all be over.

Christmas had come and gone. It was the sixth one for us in this endless war. My thoughts had returned to December of 1939, when I was in England, helping Miss Morling with the Christmas decorations, while thinking with sadness of the Hanukkah festivities of my youth. Was Miss Morling still alive? What about all of my family and friends in Rotterdam? I became quite melancholy as I was thinking of my mother, and I could not wait for December to be over.

The Germans became more and more frantic. Their ordinances had become even more nonsensical. One of their orders in the newspapers instructed people to turn in doorknobs consisting of metal, metal handles from furniture, metal housewares, garden tools, and other metal items. Of course, the ordinance was accompanied by the usual threats.

The river was frozen stiff. Since I had my fake identity papers, and I was the "niece" of the family, I often went skating with Corrie, usually at dusk. For a short while I could divert my mind and dream of being free.

And finally, December was gone and the New Year of 1945 had begun. What would it bring? Would we spend another year in hiding? It seemed like an eternity of waiting and hoping. The grain was helping us all to endure and stay alive. And so we kept praying that the Almighty would fulfill the wishes of our hearts.

Chapter 38: The Story of the Three Horses

Around the first week in February, Pa and Moe told us that they wanted to go away for one day to visit their family in Amsterdam, whom they had not seen for several years. They asked us if we could manage by ourselves. We courageously said, "Yes, of course," although deep in my heart I was worried. Of course I was happy for them that they would get to see their loved ones after all that had transpired. Felix emphasized that they should not be concerned about us and that we would be fine. Pa said, "You know, I heard through the grapevine" (he always used the term "grapevine"; he never mentioned the resistance), "that the SS and the Gestapo in the office across the river have taken to their heels. But still," he continued, "stay on your guard just the same."

That Sunday morning, the entire family left: Pa, Moe, Hannie, Bert, and Corrie. The big house felt totally abandoned somehow. First of all, Kazan, the dog, was no longer there. He disappeared one day and never came back. We had depended on him because we recognized the tone of his bark when strangers were downstairs. Another concern was that we did not know the neighbors. That is, they said hello when we were together in the air raid shelter; they seemed to tolerate us, but they never asked questions or spoke to us. I had found it strange to meet those people, and I never knew exactly who they were.

Felix said, "Let's stay upstairs. If something happens, then we are close to our hiding place." I agreed. The big window in the attic gave us ample chance to view the area. A few hours went by. Felix was writing and I was dozing off, when we heard a noise. I ran to the window and suddenly saw two Germans going around the house. I motioned to Felix, who immediately went into his hiding cell in the ceiling. I quickly threw a rug over the cell, and in a dream-state, I went down the steps and into the kitchen.

After a few minutes, the Germans began battering on the door. What to do? My brain began to work overtime. If I did not answer, they might kick the door in. I was left but one choice: open the door. I quickly ran to the front door, opened it, stepped out, and quickly closed it behind me.

There I was, face to face with the two Germans. I hastily looked at their uniforms. Thank goodness, there were no dreaded SS or Gestapo insignias on them. They were ordinary German soldiers. One of them was very tall. If he had not been the enemy, I could have classified him as handsome. The shorter one looked a bit dumb. I did not like the way that the tall one looked at me. He lifted his hand to his cap politely and said, "We need horses; are there any around here? Where are they?"

I nodded and quickly put on my wooden shoes, which stood outside the door. I started to walk toward the meadow that was situated beyond the body of water; the two Germans were following me from behind. I could understand what they were saying while they were talking to each other. I heard them comment about my wooden shoes; the shoes prevented me from walking as fast as I would have liked to. I was shivering badly, both from emotional turmoil and from the cold. In my haste I had forgotten to take my coat.

I finally reached the meadow where I knew the horses were. One of them looked old and quite exhausted. I did not know who the owner of the horses was, but to get rid of the Germans I told the two soldiers to go ahead and take them. The two men talked awhile between themselves, the tall one all the time looking at me in a flirtatious manner. Silently, I prayed very hard that they would go away and leave me alone. Finally, they slowly walked to the horses and each of them took one. The tall one clicked his heels and saluted, and then the two of them disappeared through a path back beyond the meadow. The entire episode was bizarre to me. Had they only known they had saluted a Jewish girl!

When they were out of sight, I ran toward the house and up the stairs to the attic, and called out to Felix to come out of the hiding place. I told him what had happened. He had been terribly worried, especially because I had been gone for such a long time. Yet another frightening situation in our years of hiding was over.

When the Hornsvelds returned, we were overjoyed to have the family back again. We waited awhile before telling them what had transpired while they were gone. I said, "I saw no other way out but to let them have the horses." Pa answered, "What the heck, don't worry, you did the right thing. I know who the horses belong to. But there is not enough food for them anyway. The Moffen can feed them better than we can." Pa added, as he looked at my guilt-stricken face, "It's only the horses. Let's be glad it was not you." And with that, the incident was discussed no further.

Around that time I noticed that Moe was cooking much more than usual. I did not ask any questions. But one day, Hannie came over to us and said, "Have you noticed that Moe is cooking all of the time?" "Yes," I answered, "but I don't know why." "I will tell you, but it is strictly confidential," he said.

Hannie, Felix, and I went upstairs where we could be alone, and when we sat down we could hardly wait for Hannie to start talking. Without any prelude he said, "Moe is cooking for the paratroopers." Felix and I must have looked puzzled because we asked, "What paratroopers?"

"Pa and some others rescued nineteen paratroopers; they are hidden behind the dockyard." Our mouths fell open in surprise. "Yes," Hannie continued. "We are getting fisherman's outfits for them; then they will be transported to the coast." Hannie apparently relished in our astonishment, and we could tell that he was happy to tell us about it, knowing the secret was safe with us. I asked naively, "Who will pick them up?" "Don't you know that Holland has secret connections with the Allies?" he asked. "Especially with England." Hannie always had a big smile on his face, just like his sister Corrie.

He continued his conversation with much gusto. "All will be over soon—the resistance is being supplied with lots of weapons. The Allies are dropping them off at secret places here in Holland, and when our liberators come, then we Dutch can help them with all of our weapons."

We truly needed time to digest all of this. Neither Pa, Moe, nor Bertus would ever openly discuss these things. But we were grateful to Hannie for confiding in us; it gave us a big boost. We asked him, "How will the paratroopers get to the coast and where will they be dropped off?"

"I know about the general plan but not the details," he answered. "Usually somewhere near Scheveningen at secret places. The resistance has radio contact with the Allies. They know that we Dutch are reliable and that we can be trusted." As Hannie left, he placed his finger over his lips and whispered, "They know that we can keep our mouths shut."

After he was gone, I said to Felix, "Well, well, well! Things sure look better now. I feel truly encouraged." Felix, down to earth as always, admonished me by saying, "We are not there yet; much can still happen. But," he added, "things do look much better."

And indeed, that same night we heard on the crystal all of the important events that were taking place. The Allies had cleared the west bank of the river De Roer, and they had captured the city of Cologne. Our joy overtook the fear we had for the Germans, who kept bragging—against reality—about their imaginary victories.

Just a few days later, at six o'clock in the morning, all of us in the house were awakened by the sound of a voice through a loudspeaker. It was a German shouting, "All men in the family must come forward and report." He repeated these words over and over. Pa came running in his pajamas to the attic where Bertus and Felix were sleeping. With an alarmed look on his face, he uttered, "Hey boys, can you hear it? There is a rot-mof downstairs. What should we do?" Felix got up and, looking through the window, said with a stern tone, "We must do nothing! The end of the war is near and we are not giving up now. Let's just ignore it."

As the soldier walked farther down through the area, his shouting faded away in the distance. Apparently, no one in the neighborhood paid any attention. Soon, the whole ordeal was over. But to be on the safe side, the boys stayed put inside the house. My ice skating with Corrie ended also. We all pledged to be extra careful, especially because we felt that freedom was near.

Later that month we learned that Himmler, the butcher of Europe, had tried to negotiate peace with Great Britain and the United States. But the Allies demanded that all German troops surrender on all fronts.

Chapter 39: The Broken Chain

The month of March had started with good news about the war. Finland had declared war on Germany, and the Russian armies swept into eastern Hungary. They had joined forces with Yugoslavia, swinging north and capturing Vienna and eastern Austria. The Red Army had crashed into Warsaw and Krakow.

Felix continued to write fervently in his diary, leaving out no details. The news about the war had become so exciting that the people in Holland became bolder by the day. Secrets that could never have been told before now came to light. The Dutch, known for their restrained and somewhat sober nature—not sensationalistic—now came out of their shell. They talked openly, and there seemed to be no holding back.

Around the third week in March, Piet came to see us, as he did from time to time. Although I was upstairs, I recognized his voice immediately, and when I came down, I saw him talking to Pa in the hallway. I detected a tone of excitement in their voices as Pa called out to me, "Marietje, go and get Jan. We have great news for you." In the excitement of the moment, I naively thought that they had found my mother. I ran up the stairs to get Felix. I shouted, "Come quick, there is great news!" I threw my hands up in the air, mumbling incoherently to myself, "What can it be? What is it? Oh, God, please let it be my mother . . . "

When we entered the large room, Moe was also there. Piet looked at me with that special gleam in his eye that I knew so well. As he put his pipe in the ashtray, he took my hands in his and said, "I found your brother Ies and his wife." I could not absorb this incredible news at first. My mouth fell open. I managed to ask, "Where are they? Are they all right? What happened?"

Piet, always under control, said calmly, "They are not well. The people with whom they have been hiding are completely out of food. They cannot possibly shelter them any longer." As Piet continued smoking his pipe, I lamented, "Oh, my God, oh, goodness, can we see them? And what about my sister and her husband?" I continued to jabber, looking from one person to another. Felix held me tight, trying to calm me down. Pa said, "Piet will tell us everything, and then we can see if there is anything we can do to help." I sat down, pretending to be calm, as Piet began to talk.

"I heard from friends of the neighbors that your brother and his wife are hiding with the family Veenhuizen on Het Havik, right near here," he said. We knew where Het Havik was. Of all things, on that notorious day of our visit to the Brandsens, we must have passed the very house.

Piet continued, "Your family is not well and we must move them." He then divulged that Ies and Bep were hidden in a small space in the attic and that the family needed a ladder to get them food after opening a trap door. As for using the bathroom, my brother and his wife had to knock and wait for someone to come with a ladder to let them out. They had not been out of this hole for all of these years.

Moe, being the wonderfully practical person that she was, said, "The first thing we have to do is get food to them. I'll tell Corrie to bring it there." Moe then motioned to me, "Come on Marietje, let's go to the kitchen. In the meantime, let them decide what should be done next." In the kitchen, Moe selected some nourishing food items, and we began to cook a meal. When the food was ready, Moe handed me a large tin. She said, "Try to get everything in while I get Corrie ready and tell her where to go and what to say."

When Corrie came into the room, she was already wrapped in warm clothes, holding the large can. Piet gave her the exact address and instructed her as to what to say. I had wanted to write a letter to my brother to accompany the food, but they all advised me against it. Corrie was instructed to ring the doorbell and say, "Here is food for you and for the family upstairs, from their sister." She was not to divulge who she was or where she lived.

As Corrie left, Piet said in his colorful way, "I'll be damned if a lot of Germans are not already out of here. They must know that the Canadians are pulling up to the north. Every person who has his head together knows by now that it won't be long until the Moffen are gone."

As he began to smoke his pipe again, in walked the family Brandt, as fate would have it. They had come regularly to pick up wheat, which the boys continued to courageously take through the tunnel during the night. Throughout the last two years, thanks to Pa and his connections, we also had plenty of sugar beets. They not only provided some variety in our meals, but they helped us to maintain some energy.

All of us were now in the room, talking excitedly about the upcoming troops. The conversation then shifted to the news about my brother and his wife. Piet repeated everything to the family Brandt. They listened attentively and shook their heads in sympathy, all the while looking at Felix and me.

Suddenly, Aunt Rika turned to her husband with a pleading look on her face and said, "Henk, can't we take them in? We can make room for them upstairs." Uncle Henk did not hesitate for one moment and replied, nodding to his wife, "No problem at all. It is fine with me. We have to help those poor people. Imagine living in a hole for all that time." It was a moment never to be forgotten; how lucky we were to encounter such generous, altruistic people whenever a crisis arose.

All of us waited for Corrie to come back, and when she finally returned we wanted to know exactly what had happened. In her own charming way, she calmly said, "It went fine. After I rang the bell, a woman opened the door and I said what you told me to say. There was nothing to it. She took the can and thanked me. I'm sure she understood what it was all about."

All of us were elated that everything had gone well. I gave Corrie a big hug, and Felix and I thanked everyone from the depths of our hearts. As we all got up to leave, Piet said, "Henk and I will work something out, and I promise you that it will be soon."

Through Pa and the Van den Hoeven family, we had continued to maintain some regular contact with Felix's family. But this situation with my brother was different; although we knew my family members had been found, we could not contact them or see them. We just had to be patient, to wait, and to trust in fate.

After a few days had passed with Corrie bringing food to the home on Het Havik on a regular basis, Pa said to us, "It is time to take your family to Rika and Henk. They are ready for them. I discussed everything with Piet—how to go about getting them there safely."

I had spent much time pondering when my brother and his wife would go to Henk and Rika's. How would things work out? Would they be safe? I tried hard to maintain my composure at all times, careful not to reveal my anxiety. I remembered my excitement, my fears, and my hopes when Piet was to take my mother to a safe hiding place and how desperate I became when things had gone wrong. I had never gotten over that tragedy, and I knew that for the rest of my life I never would.

But at the end of that week just as I had calmed down, both Felix and I were upstairs when Pa came into the room. He had a look on his face that seemed to say something good had occurred. And it certainly had! As he sat down on the bed, he said with no preamble, "Your brother and his wife

Pa Hornsveld with his sister Rika

are now safe with Henk and Rika." I stared at him, at first with disbelief that all had gone so well. Then I went over to him and hugged him tightly. The questions then tumbled out of my mouth, "How, when, how are they . . . ?"

He said, "Take it easy; they are fine now. I went last night to the family on Het Havik. I told them that I knew about the hiding of Ies and Bep and that I knew of another place for them. The family was agreeable; they trusted me. They got your brother and his wife down the ladder. I put them at ease and we walked slowly to Rika and Henk's home, where they are now safe." Pa made it all sound so easy, although in our hearts we knew that it must have been a dangerous and complicated ordeal.

I asked, "How do they look and are they okay?" Pa winked his eye and said in a typical uncomplicated Dutch way, "Well, they don't particularly look as if they came from a health resort, but I can assure you that they will be all right again." And with that, he left our room.

Felix consoled me as I began to cry. He took me in his arms and said, "Let's be grateful for these wonderful people; we must pray that the Almighty will continue to bestow his blessings on them." We sat there in that small room for a long time in complete silence, both absorbed in our own thoughts, yet both thinking the same thing: when will it finally be over?

THE END OF THE ROAD

Chapter 40: Mission Impossible

There was so much news on the crystal radio and so many events that took place in April, one after the other, that it was almost impossible to keep up with everything. The confusion and tension were growing by the day.

We all realized that we needed to get rid of the dreaded Germans as soon as possible, lest we all die of starvation. Food rations had been minimized to half a loaf of bread per person per week, along with a small portion of meat.

We counted ourselves lucky to have some wheat left. It had become impossible for the boys to go through the tunnel any longer, because lately, we had seen a great number of German soldiers in our area.

On April 12, 1945, we heard the sad news on the crystal radio that the American president, Franklin D. Roosevelt, had died. All of us were in shock. Pa said, "What a blow . . . I feel as if it were a personal loss that this had to happen just now." Our joy over the impending liberation was severely tempered.

Later that week, we suddenly heard loud shooting outside. The sound set me back to that horrible day of May 10, 1940, when I woke up to the same sound, when the Germans invaded our country. All of us dressed quickly and came together in the large room. Looking out of the window, we saw a great number of German soldiers running toward the house. They began to bang on the door and yell loudly. At first, we all huddled together in fear for our lives. Finally, Pa went and opened the front door. A German officer screamed, "Aus, aus, Alle muessen heraus, schnell, schnell!" Translated, this means, "Out, out, everybody must go out, quick, quick!"

We all ran into the air raid shelter amidst the heavy shooting which was taking place right over our heads. It turned out that the Canadians were already in the area, on one side of the river, shooting at the Germans who were on the other side. The noise was deafening with planes flying low. The end was so near and yet, the question was *would we be able to survive?*

It was a chaotic situation and we could not quite figure out what was going on. The firing at times tapered, and during those times, if we did not see any Germans, we took those opportunities to run back to the house to fetch some food and personal belongings. We realized that we had to stay in the air raid shelter as we heard the Germans shouting and yelling nervously at the top of their lungs. The time dragged on slowly as we contemplated what we should do.

Night came and we realized that there was nothing for us to do but stay in the shelter. Sometimes, as we sat leaning against each other, a few of us would lie down. Occasionally, Hannie stuck his head out of the entrance of the shelter to survey the situation. Each time he came down, he reported that there were still Germans around. Hunger pangs had set in. Corrie moaned, "Moe, I am hungry." It had been a full day and night that we had been cooped up in the shelter.

The next morning, as dawn broke, Hannie suddenly turned to Pa and Bertus, and with a look of expectation in his eyes he said, "Pa, we might have a way out. Do you remember the circus wagon that belongs to Hammersen and Vermolen? It is still stored away down beyond the dockyard." Pa nodded slowly and said, "What about it?" "Well," continued Hannie, "I remember that the helper of Bakker had told me that he still takes care of that old horse that is nearby in the barn. We cannot possibly survive in this hole here, and who knows for how long this will go on? Let's try to take the wagon and the horse and get out of here."

Pa carefully thought through the idea. After all, he had the responsibility for his family and for Felix and me. Moe and Bertus remarked, "What, for heaven's sake, are we to do? We cannot possibly stay here. One way or the other, our lives are at stake." Bertus added with a tone of urgency, "Yes, Pa, it is our last chance. The Canadians are here already." Pa, still pondering this dangerous idea, said to no one in particular, "Where can we go with that old horse?" Moe answered, "Well, all I can think of is going to Rika and Henk." We knew they lived at the opposite end of our town, quite far from where we were.

The conversation continued back and forth among us. We talked a lot about the pros and cons of taking the circus truck and the horse, until Felix spoke. He said, "We must take a chance; it is the only hope for survival. We are in the midst of a battle. The Germans are very nervous, and they might kill us and no one would know. We have to find a way out."

Finally, we all agreed to do everything possible to escape from the dreaded air raid shelter. Hannie and Bertus were ready to get to work immediately. Felix said, "Please let me go with you, I know all about horses; I was raised on a farm." But Pa, still having the fear of hiding fresh in his mind, said, "Jan, you better stay with us for now; you can help later."

And so the two boys left the shelter amidst the fighting, leaving the rest of us in a terrific state of tension. We were on pins and needles; I prayed silently, asking God for their safe return. We pretended to be calm, but I knew that our thoughts were spinning wildly like windmills. We had horrible visions of what could happen. The waiting seemed to last an eternity; no one spoke a word. Just as Felix mentioned, "I'll go and see what's going on," the boys came back into the shelter. They shouted excitedly over the tumult, "We got the wagon and the horse, come quickly!" As we ran out of the shelter, Hannie shouted, "We had a darned job getting that horse ready and getting the harness over his head."

We ran through the lumberyard and, indeed, there it was: the circus wagon and the old horse hitched in front of the carriage. We stepped in quickly while the Germans and Canadians were shooting at each other across the river. Felix took the horse by the reins, trying to calm it down. Amid the fury of the fighting we left in the direction of the Brandt home, with Felix leading the horse as he walked beside the wagon.

The poor horse trotted very slowly. We could tell that it was afraid of the noise and not used to being out. It often pulled its ears down, not wanting to continue on.

We used back roads to avoid the fighting. It turned out to be a long, long trip—it seemed as if it would never end. We also realized what a risk we were taking. The situation had a horrendous impact on our nerves—we knew we could be shot at any minute!

Finally we reached the home of the Brandt family. We rang the bell and, as we stepped in, they were flabbergasted to see us step out of a circus wagon and into their home!

Aunt Rika threw up her hands into the air and shouted, "Oh, my God, oh, my goodness, what's happened! Come in, come in!" She stumbled over her words, adding breathlessly, "We will be liberated. Oh, goodness, what a world we live in!"

Her husband took it more calmly. He said, "Sit down, sit down, let's hear what happened." Turning to his wife, he said, "Rika, get Ies and Bep here; boy, oh, boy, will they ever be surprised to see their family here!"

After a few minutes, my brother and his wife came into the room. My heart began to pound. I was elated beyond words to be reunited with my oldest brother and my sister-in-law. The years of slaughter, persecutions, and hiding had left their mark on them, I could see. I noticed in a flash how poorly they looked, so aged and ailing. But then we flew into each other's arms, crying and laughing at the same time. We hugged and kissed and could not speak for a while.

As the emotion of the moment began to calm a little, Aunt Rika said, "You all look downright exhausted and beat up; but we are dying to know what happened." After we were settled in, Pa began to relate the story of our escape and how the boys courageously had gone to the dockyard to get the circus wagon and the old horse. He told of our flight—our painfully slow one—amidst the fierce battle. The more Pa talked, the more we realized how we had gambled with our lives in a desperate attempt for survival and freedom.

Another miracle had taken place; we had once again accomplished a "mission impossible." All we could do now was wait for the end of this miserable war.

Chapter 41: The Miracle of Liberation

As I look back now, I see that it is difficult to believe that thirteen people managed to live in the small home of the Brandt family. The greatest part of that time was spent near the crystal radio, which was hidden upstairs. Some of us slept on the floor or we slept together in a bed. Some of us kept our ears glued to the crystal radio, not wanting to miss a minute of the news, which continued to be broadcast day and night. I remember sharing a bed with the Brandt children, as we tried to sleep with our clothes on. The airplanes were flying so low we could almost see the pilots. Pa said, "Don't worry, these are Allied planes; they are throwing weapons out."

Around the end of April, Felix and Pa came running into the bedroom. They were nearly out of breath from excitement. Felix managed to say, "Listen to this! The Italian partisans have captured Mussolini. They have shot him and his mistress somewhere in Switzerland." Pa added, catching his breath, "Boy, oh, boy, and the Russian units are already on the Elbe River." There was so much good news that all of us were upbeat. There was hardly time to prepare food. The incredible events reported in the news overtook everything, even our hunger pangs.

The climax came on April 30, 1945. I was dozing off with some people in the same bed as the men came in screaming at us to wake up. They yelled, "Hitler and his mistress Eva Braun are dead!" Henk Brandt, with his hand waving in the air, began to dance around, screaming, "Finally, finally, we will get rid of those bastards."

None of us could sleep that night. When we calmed down a bit, we learned that Hitler and Eva Braun had committed suicide. Of course, the Germans still denied it. They maintained that Hitler had died defending Berlin, and that he had named Admiral Karl Doenitz as his successor!

But of course, the BBC confirmed that after the suicide their bodies had been burned.

In the excitement of all this good news, the family wanted to raise the Dutch flag, but there were warnings on the radio not to be too hasty and to stay inside our homes for safety. The tension was enormous throughout Holland; it built by the hour.

A friend of Pa, who was from the resistance, came to our home the next day. He told us that they were preparing to arrest members of the NSB especially the NSB mayor of Amersfoort. They were waiting for the Canadians to come in to arrest the war criminals. But the Germans did not give up. When they were told that they had to capitulate, the German commandant maintained that the rumors were false and that it was only Waffen Ruhe (Armistice).

If the circumstances had not been so serious at that time, one could have compared the thirteen of us as being in a stage play. All of us were mad with jubilation; we were talking nonsense and talking quite loudly. No whispering for us any longer! Each one of us came forward with the craziest remarks, not realizing what we were saying. The Dutch language is filled with very spicy but good-natured expressions. For instance, I remember vividly how Pa said, in an agitated manner, "For Pete's sake, what the hell is going on, are we free or not? What is the matter with those German clowns? Don't they know by now that they are not welcome here any longer?"

Suddenly Moe, who spoke very seldom, supported her husband's anger by saying, "Yes, what are they doing here anyway?"

And so, everyone had his or her say; all were swept up by the circumstances. Then, on Friday night, May 4, 1945, we heard people running jubilantly in the streets, yelling, "There is peace, peace; the surrender goes in tomorrow morning!" We ran to listen to the radio because we weren't sure if it was true. After all, the curfew was still on. Or was it? It seemed as if nobody thought any longer of the so-called Sperr Stunden, that horrible German word for curfew hours.

However, our joy did not last long. At eleven o'clock at night, the Germans came unexpectedly, shooting their way through the streets. All of us dashed inside, totally confused and appalled at the same time. In no time the streets were again silent.

The next day, Saturday, May 5, the uncertainty got the better of us. The radio announced that we had to wait for the Allied troops to come in. We didn't know what was going on. The German military was still standing guard. The SS police still occupied bridges, were still arresting citizens, and seemed to still be shooting to their hearts' content. Uncle Henk said, "Aren't the Moffen ever going to give up? What poor losers!"

And so it went: our expectations were back to point zero once more. Flags had to be taken in, and the Germans again seemed to be in control. Hannie said, "We have to wait until we get rid of those hated German uniforms. I don't ever want to see them again."

It was clear that the Germans themselves did not know what was going on. One group of their armed forces seemed to know that they had to give up, and another group claimed that there was only an armistice.

Suddenly, late that night, Bertus, Hannie, and Felix came running down the stairs, gesturing wildly and stumbling over their words, shouting, "There is unconditional surrender! The Germans have surrendered!" One of the boys tried to sing the Dutch National Anthem! All of us became hysterical. As others came down the stairs, we hugged them, they hugged us, we kissed them, they kissed us, we cried, we screamed, we fell over each other. I cannot fully describe that eventful, glorious night.

My sister-in-law became somewhat crazy; I was worried about her. She kept screaming at the top of her lungs, running in and out of the house, her face turning red, then blue. She yelled, "Where is the flag? We have to put the garbage out . . . " She continued to utter total nonsense. She clearly could not restrain herself. All of the agony over the past five years had come to a climax.

Amidst the screaming and the yelling, Felix took me into his arms. While we embraced, he uttered over and over again, with tears streaming down his face, "We made it, we made it, thank God we made it." We stood there for a while, trying to realize that we were truly free.

Then, Uncle Henk Brandt left the room. After a while he returned carrying two bottles of Dutch gin. As he smiled broadly, he said, "Let's have a good one and get drunk! I hid these two bottles and saved them all these darned years just for this occasion." Despite our empty stomachs, we drank "a good one." I lost my balance and fell under the table, but it was worth it!

Then we went upstairs to listen to the small crystal radio that had served us well on so many occasions and saved us from desperation and thoughts of giving up. We learned that on Monday, May 7, 1945, German General Alfred Jodl of the German High Command had entered the Allied Headquarters in Reims, France, and there, in a red school building, had signed the terms of the unconditional surrender on behalf of his government. General Eisenhower's Chief of Staff, General Walter Smith, had signed for the Allies.

On May 9, 1945, Berlin ratified the surrender terms. After five years and eight months, the European phase of this horrible war had ended. My country, the Netherlands, was liberated by the Canadians under General Henry Crerar, and on May 9 the word went forth: HOLLAND IS FREE!

The Dutch authorities immediately issued an ordinance, admonishing the Germans not to shoot while leaving and that if they did continue to shoot weapons at the Dutch civilians, they would be considered war criminals and arrested. Shortly thereafter, Queen Wilhelmina, her daughter Juliana, and her husband Prince Bernhard, along with their four children returned to Holland.

For us, the next phase was where to go, what to do, and how to find the rest of our family members.

Queen Wilhelmina returns to Holland

Chapter 42: The Reunion

We had not seen any Canadians in our area, and we very much wanted to go out into the streets. But it was already near midnight, and Pa said, "Listen, all of us desperately need some rest. Let's try to get some sleep and leave early tomorrow morning." Moe agreed with him. She added, "We must go and see if our house is still there. And you, Jan and Marietje, have to go to the Van den Hoevens' and get together with your family, while Bep and Ies have to go to see about their store." Aunt Rika nodded in agreement. She remarked, "I know that none of us can sleep, but we must at least rest for a few hours and gather some strength."

They were right. All of us felt emotionally and physically drained, especially after those drinks, the "good ones," as Uncle Brandt called them. We were too tired to even take off our clothes, and we fell down wherever there was room. We were all totally exhausted.

Early the next morning we went out on the street. What a sensation! We still could not believe that we were free. As we saw the Germans leaving, a lot of people shouted obscenities at them. Some Dutch people even wanted to get into physical fights with the Germans. The family Hornsveld left at the same time we did, and then Felix, Ies, Bep, and I were on our way. We planned to first go to the Van den Hoevens' and see Felix's family.

Suddenly, we heard from far off a dull droning sound. The sound came closer and closer. Our first reaction was, "Seek shelter!" But then we saw hundreds of people standing on the rooftops of houses, cheering wildly and shouting with joy, waving at the airplanes. Felix took a good look and shouted over the noise, "Oh, my word, they are Lancasters! They are throwing food items from the planes."

Now we could clearly see the planes soaring stately over the neighboring towns and villages. The people became almost hysterical. They wanted to know where the food was—food that we had all needed for so long. Then some organizers called out that we had to wait just awhile longer until the food could be properly distributed.

Winding our way through the throngs of people, we finally reached the Van den Hoevens. All of us at that point were in fair condition, but at least we were alive. When we entered the home, Felix's mother was clutching her prayer book in her hand; Mrs. Van den Hoeven said, "Your mother would not let go of it all of these years."

We stayed there for quite a while, then my brother was eager to go to his store. And so the four of us took off again. On our way, we passed thousands of people dancing in the streets, some of them singing our national anthem, "Het Wilhelmus." At times, we stood still and joined in. It was all very moving, almost surreal. Flags were waving all over: British flags, American flags, Canadian flags, and, of course, Dutch flags. Everyone wore orange ribbons, orange shawls, orange buttons—the color orange was the Dutch national symbol of the House of Orange. There was even a man on the street handing out flyers with the words to the American national anthem, neatly typed in English, with the Dutch translation typed underneath! I had wondered how he had gotten these.

It took a long, long time to push our way through the enthusiastic crowds. But finally we reached the street we were looking for, called Het Hof. Lo and behold, the store was still there, albeit changed on both the inside and the outside.

The next thing we knew, a man who owned the business next to my brother's appeared; I remembered him well from before the war. His name was Mr. Veenendaal. He ran over to Ies, and gave him a huge, heart-filled bear hug. He then embraced the rest of us. This neighbor used to run an art shop next to my brother's delicatessen. He said to us, "Let me get some chairs; we'll sit and I'll tell you what happened." After we were seated, he began to explain how he had fooled the Germans by wallpapering the entire store. He had taken out all of my brother's equipment and stored it away, replacing the equipment with his own art materials.

He finished his story and turned to my brother and said, "You know, Cohen, I am a good Christian and I prayed every day that some how, some day, you'd come back. Thanks to the good Lord, by golly, here you are. Welcome back." While my brother wiped the tears from his eyes, my sister-in-law and I began to cry. We were moved by this man's concern and caring for my brother.

As we were still talking with this neighbor, two events happened that I still consider nothing less than miracles. Even the most well-made movie with a powerful ending could not compare to this.

The five of us were quite wrapped up in our conversation, so much so that we had not seen them coming. But then, my heart began to pound as I turned and saw my sister and her husband; they seemed to appear out of nowhere. I saw at a glance how terribly sick my sister's husband looked. While my sister did not look too bad, I noticed that she had lost a lot of weight and her beauty was gone.

But what a reunion it was! We flew into each other's arms, our emotions soaring, the words tumbling out of our mouths asking questions. We wanted to know everything all at once from one another. Finally, I learned that they had found shelter with a farming family in Hoogland, a neighboring village. They had spent their days and nights in a loft in the barn, sleeping with the cows and horses.

When I think of the next miracle that took place, it still causes me to get goose bumps. We were all talking animatedly. I then noticed a young man, dressed in a military uniform, coming around the corner of the street, walking slowly toward us. There was something familiar in his step, and I thought to myself, he looks like my brother Ben; but no, that cannot be. I thought I was delusional, the effects of many years of hiding. As this young man came closer, I became convinced that in all of the excitement I had lost my mind. He looked so much like Ben.

Then my sister ran to him, screaming, "It is Ben; oh, my God, it is Ben! Ben is back, Ben, Ben, oh, Ben!" I stood there, immobilized, thinking, "Am I dreaming?" I remember the stripes on my brother's uniform. The neighbor came with some water, and my brother embraced me! Ies repeated over and over, "How is it possible? Where were you all of these years? With what units . . . in what army?" He went on and on with the same questions. After I gained my sense of reality, I noticed how handsome my brother looked in his colorful uniform, which was decorated with a number of medals.

Mr. Veenendaal seemed to fully understand our emotional state. He said, "This I want to hear. I must hear what happened." Then several more people came over to where we were standing, and in no time a small crowd had assembled to find out who this military man was.

My brother, who was humble in his ways and keenly intelligent, was a man of few words. But he realized that he owed an explanation. He related in very few words how he had left Holland in May of 1940, riding his bike into Belgium. There, close friends had helped him through France, where other business relations had gotten him over the Pyrenees Mountains and into Spain.

In Spain, Ben had contacted the Dutch Embassy and indicated that he wanted to join the Allied army. After they had checked him out thoroughly, he was sent to England where he was trained and later joined the Allied troops in the Princess Irene Brigade. He fought his way through Normandy. He was one of our liberators in the south of Holland, where he had been for one year. He had served as a translator—my brother spoke several languages fluently—and also worked in the intelligence units.

Ben told his story in a simple way, not making much ado about it. He finished by saying how enormously happy he was to find us, especially since his superior officer had said to him, "Listen, Cohen, don't expect to find any of your family members alive." Yet, his intuition brought him to my oldest brother's store.

We all stood there fascinated with my brother's story. I knew that at some time we had to talk about what happened to our mother and our other family members from Amersfoort. I dreaded having to relive that horrible evening when the Nazis picked up my mother and deported her. I simply could not bear to discuss that day of hell.

Felix held my hand and took over. He spoke about how things had gone terribly wrong for my mother and later for the aunt and uncle whom we all

My brother Ben

had loved so much. He told them how we had gotten married by Mr. Van Dam and that we had been the last couple in that small Synagogue. He discussed how so many of our friends had been taken away by the Nazis, and he related the death of my Uncle Isse. Felix talked about Piet and the Hornsvelds. The people surrounding us, total strangers, occasionally shook their heads in disbelief. Some of them began to curse those "damned and cruel Germans."

When I look back on it now, I realize how strange the situation was that day. There stood my brother, our liberator, and the six of us, surrounded by total strangers who evidently took great interest in all that we were talking about.

A long time had passed, and then suddenly we heard loud cheering and shouting coming from the main street of the town. The Canadians had finally arrived in their cars and jeeps! My sister was the first to run out into the street with all of us following her and the crowd of people running behind us.

Coming to the main street, called De Lange Straat, a spectacle unfolded that I will never forget. There was no holding back any longer. The Canadians, in their impressive uniforms, looking healthy and well nourished, must have been overwhelmed. Young people literally stormed onto the cars and jeeps; flowers flew all over the streets. People surrounded the columns, throwing streamers, flags, cheering, waving, and becoming wild. At one point, we could not even see the Canadians because everyone was jumping on their cars. We later heard a Canadian ask, "Are these the restrained Dutch?" The Dutch had expressed their exuberance!

I kept thinking, "How full of changes and uncertainties is life. One minute there is sadness, the next minute happiness. Everything seems to be intertwined." My thoughts went to all those who had been deported. What had happened to them? Are they coming back? When will we know? My thoughts then returned to Mr. Van Dam's words: "There is a time for crying, a time for laughing, a time for grief and a time for joy. God brings everything to pass precisely at its time . . . "

Felix and me after the war, before going to America

EPILOGUE

Though the Germans had left my country in a tremendous mess, the Dutch spirit was soaring. I remember that one of the first restorations was changing the streets back to their original names. On several occasions, these changes were accompanied by religious ceremonies. At the same time, all signs that the Germans so maliciously had put up to eliminate the Jewish population in Holland were removed, and all traffic and directional indicators in the German language were taken away.

After five years of war, destruction, terror, and starvation, the Dutch had a tremendous task ahead of them to rebuild their country. All laws that the German "High Command" had instituted during their occupation were immediately canceled. The cities and harbors had to be rebuilt, and food distribution had to be organized. The health and school systems had to be raised to meet prewar standards.

Food and clothing were brought to us in abundant quantities. America and Sweden were sending loads of food, clothing, and various items whose existence had been completely forgotten. All Holland had banners raised with the slogan: Amerika Helpt (America Helps). The Jewish Joint Distribution Committee of America had also set up locations and depots to deliver kosher food, clothing, toiletries, shoes, and stockings. Even prayer books and other religious items were made available to us.

Memorial services were held in the various cities and towns for the many victims of the war, for the fallen heroes of the resistance, and for the Jewish citizens who had been so brutally deported and who had perished at the hands of the Nazis. A very special day was set aside on May 12, 1945, for the Jewish citizens who were still alive. According to the newspapers, out of approximately 140,000 Dutch Jews, only 6,000 had survived.

For the first time in all of the years of terror for the Jewish people of Holland, Shabbat services were held in makeshift Synagogues in ambulances donated by the Jewish population of England. These services were frequently attended by Canadian officers of the Jewish faith, as well as members of the Princess Irene Brigade.

In spite of all I had been through, all I had witnessed over the dreadful years of the ruthless German occupation, I still entertained a flicker of hope to one day hear from my mother. It was too soon to contact the Red Cross, although we all tried hard to find out information about our loved ones and what had happened to them.

But shortly after the liberation, the son of my sister's husband was brought back to Amersfoort from a concentration camp. I remember he looked like a skeleton, almost unable to speak. It turned out that he and his sister had been picked up by the Germans and deported to Poland. His sister died in the camp.

The chaos in Holland was indescribable. We found out that my Aunt Sien and her youngest son, Jacob, had survived; but her oldest son, Simon, had ended up in the death camp of Auschwitz, the largest extermination camp established by Himmler in 1940. Simon, almost near death, had been liberated by the advancing Russian troops who had dropped him off at Prague, fearing that he would die on the way. He was then sent by the Red Cross to the south of France where they tried to bring him back to health. In 1946, they were able to return him to Holland.

My uncle, the chessmaster, perished in the death camp of Sobibor, and the same fate befell my relatives in Amersfoort, as well as other relatives and friends. Now we learned about the gas chambers and the many other horrid atrocities that the Germans had subjected the Jews to. When we realized the magnitude of the German crimes that they had orchestrated to reach their "Final Solution," our minds could not comprehend it. The shock was so immense that I almost went mad thinking of how my mother had found her death. It would haunt me for the rest of my life.

The news that was broadcast from the crystal radio had never mentioned anything about the fate of the Jewish people in the concentration camps. I

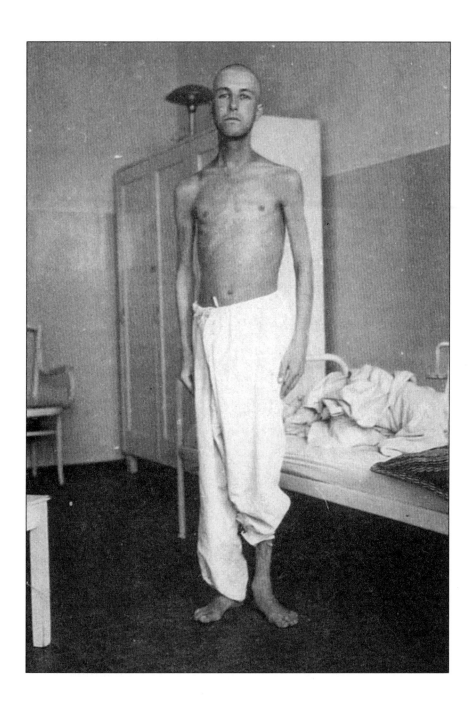

My cousin Simon de Haas survived the deathcamp of Auschwitz and was photographed while recuperating in a hospital in Buhl (halfway between France and Germany)

was desolate and cried bitterly nearly all of the time. Having gone through the war, I knew the mentality of the Germans but not to the extent of what I now heard and was reading about in the newspapers. What could have possibly brought the people of this so-called cultured nation to such hellish crimes?

After the war, Felix and I contacted the Dutch Red Cross to locate where my mother had been, and indeed we learned that my mother had faced her death exactly the day that I heard her voice call my name.

In 1946 the official letter arrived from the Red Cross confirming that my mother and all other family members and friends that we had inquired about had perished in the gas chambers of Sobibor.

We immediately began to search out where exactly Sobibor was located. We learned that it had been one of the six extermination camps in Poland, and it was situated in a wooded area near a small village by the same name in the Lublin District. At the Wannsee Conference, held in January 1942, the Germans decided to speed up the extermination of the Jewish people, and in March 1942, they began construction work on this camp to prepare for mass extermination of all Jews.

By now, we simply had to think about our future. Both the Brandsen and the Hornsveld families insisted that we stay with them for as long as we wanted. But we had to pick up the pieces of our lives and start all over. It was not easy. First we had to go to several different authorities to verify our true identities and to show proof of our time in hiding. The authorities were very helpful in this respect. Soon after, the resistance organization helped us locate a home. Through this organization, Felix's family, who wanted to stay in Amersfoort, was allotted a home in this town.

Felix, the ever-active man that he was, wanted to go back to Rotterdam. With all kinds of reference papers from the resistance, we qualified for a nice flat there. Once on our own, Felix immediately applied for Dutch citizenship, which he received in 1947.

The aftermath of our five-year ordeal was mindboggling. Once we were settled in our flat in Rotterdam, we went back to Amersfoort to see if the many documents that we had collected over the years had been saved. First,

Nr. 1025

BIJLAGEN:

TYPE: J.M.G.   J. P. A. No.

BETREFT: Informatie

BIJ BEANTWOORDING DAGTEEKENING EN NUMMER
VAN DIT SCHRIJVEN AAN TE HALEN

30 Januari 1946

den Heer F.Levi,
Brussestraat 13a,
Rotterdam.

Mijnheer,

In antwoord op Uw aanvrage van 17-12-'45 heb ik de eer
U het volgende te berichten:

	is op transport gesteld met bestemming, althans in de richting van:	datum
Aleida Cohen-van Beek geb. 23-7-80	Auschwitz	7-9-42
Flora Frank-van Beek geb. 8-9-78	Sobibor (Polen)	11-5-43
Jules Frank geb. 11-4-86	id.	id.
Ephraim de Haas geb. 28-11-87	Auschwitz	12-10-42
Carolina Salzer-Erle geb. 14-6-67	id.	id.
Bernhard Salzer geb. 24-5-63	id.	id.
Trude Hofman-Blum geb. 30-1-14	id.	31-8-42
Günther Hofmann geb. 26-4-07	id.	id.
Hertha Mannheimer geb. 6-5-91	Sobibor.	7-9-43

Daaruit komt niet bij voorbaat vast te staan, dat gezochten aldaar hun laatste verblijfplaats hebben gevonden. Immers
in vele gevallen werden gedeporteerden naar voorhands onbekende b
stemming verder gevoerd. De ervaring leert ons echter, dat op
een uitzondering, vergeleken bij het geheel, na, de kans op te-
rugkeer van gezochten zeer gering moet worden geacht.

Het onderzoek, hetwelk op grote moeilijkheden stuit, wordt
desniettemin voortgezet.

Inmiddels verblijf ik

hoogachtend,
HET NEDERLANDSCHE ROODE KRUIS
de chef der Afdeeling
Opsporing Joodsche Personen

*This is a copy of the letter we received from the Red Cross confirming the death of my mother and
other family members*

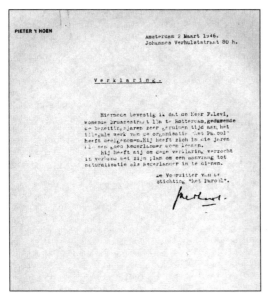

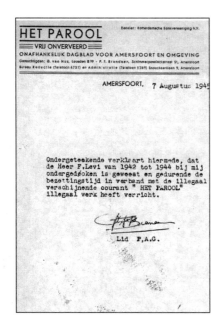

From top: Letter from Pieter 't Hoen, head of Het Parool; *letter from Piet Brandsen confirming our help in the Resistance Movement; letter of confirmation of our work with the resistance*

we went to the Brandsen family. After digging and digging in a particular spot in their yard, we found the two metal boxes and all of the documents and clippings in good condition.

From there we went to the Hornsvelds', where our diaries and other important papers were still in hiding places. We then went to Mrs. Kolkman's to look for the family photos that my mother had so reverently saved and taken to Amersfoort. They were all in good condition, as well. We were very grateful. It lifted my spirits to know that I had something from my past, especially photos from my mother, to cling to.

My sister and her husband, as well as my oldest brother and his wife, stayed in Amersfoort. Ies was able to start his business again in the same store.

In 1946, I became pregnant, but because the doctor could not make it to our home on time during my labor, our baby girl was stillborn. Both Felix and I wanted to get out of Holland, the memories weighed heavily on us. In June 1946 Felix's sister Nel gave birth to their son, Eric.

In August, Japan surrendered and everyone hoped for permanent peace in the world. But soon after, the Cold War began. We applied for a visa to go to America, but at that time there was a quota system for entrance into the United States. It would take a long time, but with the help and sponsorship of Felix's two brothers, Hugo and Sam, who had lived in New York for a number of years and served in the American army, we were hopeful to get our papers to leave Holland.

Finally, in 1948, the American Embassy furnished us with visas, and in April we left Holland to begin a new life in America. We again had to part with our families. It seemed as if we were always saying good-bye.

Nel's son Eric

I managed to take all of our documents and war papers with me to America. It was a suitcase full. In the course of the years, I kept looking at that suitcase, knowing what dismal memories it held. On many occasions I was tempted to throw out the whole thing. But in later years, I began to realize that those documents represented a piece of history that would be most important for the generations that would come after us.

It wasn't until 1984 that I slowly began to sort through and file all of the war documents in chronological order. I sometimes translated certain documents into the English language. After several years of working on the project, Felix and I were able to donate our entire collection to the United States Holocaust Memorial Museum in Washington, D.C. The curator was utterly amazed by such a large collection.

After Dina's death at a relatively young age, we invited Piet to our home in Newport Beach, California, which he visited many times. On one of his stays with us, he insisted on giving us six precious bronze medals he received from the Resistance Organization in Holland for his courageous work during the war when he had saved many lives, including ours. We later donated these medals to the Holocaust Memorial Museum. Piet died of lung cancer in 1976.

Felix's brother Sam who fought in the Aleutian Islands

Pa and Moe Hornsveld also stayed with us on several of their visits to America. Their two sons, Bertus and Hannie, immigrated to the United States in the 1950s. Bertus earned his contractor's license in America and became a well-known and well-respected builder with his own company. To our deep sorrow, Bertus passed away of lung cancer in 1996. Hannie has his own thriving business in electrical appliances in Costa Mesa, California. The two brothers built the home that Felix and I live in Newport Beach; it is still beautiful and contemporary.

My prediction about Corrie Hornsveld's talent came to pass. She is now a noted Dutch painter and received many commissions throughout the years. She is also registered with Sotheby. On one of her visits to America, she presented us with a beautiful, delicately colored landscape painting, which adorns our wall in the dining room. It represents a tranquil scene in Amersfoort and portrays figures of young people on a canal on a crisp winter day. The bare branches of the trees surrounding the canal partially conceal the stucco home, which stands in silence. It embodies a world of haunting memories during the war-torn days spanning the five years of terror.

The four Brandsen girls are still in Holland; they are all married and some of them are already grandparents. We remain in contact with all of them. To our great sorrow, Nel, the oldest, passed away unexpectedly.

After Kurt's mother passed away, Felix's family immigrated to South America, where they remained.

"Moltjeveer" (his real name was Mr. Van der Veer), whom we always visited on our trips to Holland, was very ill the last time we saw him. To our deep sorrow, he passed away soon after of lung cancer. His memory is a blessing to us.

The loss of my mother and family members weighed heavily on me. Our close-knit family had been torn apart by unspeakable crimes. Whoever was still alive ended up in different parts of the world.

I shall weep forever for the horrible fate of the millions of innocent men, women, children, and babies who were murdered by the German executioners in such abominable ways. It is my strong belief that with the destruction of the former centers of European Jewry, we should recognize the role that we must continue: To fulfill the dreams and goals of those whose voices are stilled forever.

We also must continue to strive for peace and understanding for all mankind.

Newport Beach, California, USA, June 1998.

From top: Felix and me before returning to Holland from England; "Moe" Hornsveld; Mr. and Mrs. Hornsveld with us on one of their visits to America; Mr. and Mrs. Hornsveld enjoying their visit in Newport Beach.

From top, left to right: Moe Hornsveld visiting the Van Beeks; my first visit back to Holland in 1960 with a friend; Pa Hornsveld and me on his sailboat in Holland; visiting Holland with our rescuers, Pa Hornsveld, Piet and Dina Brandsen; Piet with Felix and me on his first visit to America; honoring the Hornsveld brothers in our Synagogue, Temple Isaiah of Newport Beach

From top: Piet and me on one of his visits; the six beautiful bronze medals given to Piet for saving our lives; Felix's five diaries and my three books with hundreds of documents about the Holocaust; our diaries, books, and Piet's medals, which he gave us

Above: Piet Brandsen's first visit to America, I am holding my forged document papers
Below: My brother Ben's decorations for fighting in Normandy, 1944

From the Holocaust library of Felix and Flory Van Beek, this grievous lamentation by an unknown husband was found after the war. The Van Beeks brought it with them to America.

IN MEMORIAM
Loneliness

Your lips
Which I have kissed so much
Your hair
So dark and tousled
Your heart
Your young and tender heart
On which I rested my head
* in gentle, loving passion.*

Did it have to be this way
I ask within
For I do not know whether you
* died*
How and when—so far away.

Are you in pain
Are you in hunger
What wanderings are left to us
Before we are together again
Oh, will we be together
Again?

That early spring morning
When you left our home
Wearing your white, thin blouse
How sunny and happy you were
For neither of us heard
The soft rustlings of death
Neither of us could see
The scepter of fate
The shadowy wings of forever
Flying over your face
That turned to me
Radiantly smiling
Then.

During all those fearsome nights
And days
It seemed I detected your brisk
Light steps
Walking our stairs
And then, nothing but a single
* letter*
A dreaded form letter
Bearing your name, a stamp of
* Germany*
The barrack number that became
* your home*
And you asked for warm clothing.

My heart refused to break
Just then
Oh, not just then
For I saw you somewhere very far
Alone
Standing near a river
Was it beside the waters
* of Babylon*
Wearing a slave's chain?

If I had Aladdin's wonderlamp
And the flying carpets of the sultan
And the caliphs
I would fly the clouds of memory
Until I might descend upon your
* camp*
My arms to embrace you tightly
Never again to let you go
But to lift you to the skies
And the stars

To the islands of Epipsychidion,
Orpheus or Ogygia
To long forgotten shores
There to be together, my Calypso,
To kiss your hands
Which tended our home so
  lovingly
And then
And then, kiss your dark and
  tousled hair.

Who knows whether we will see
  each other
Again
Is there but one purpose to the tortures
To our severed threads of life
That were woven for a shattered
  fragment
Of forever?

But then
To live without a shadow of hope
Is not enough
And so we cling in dream, my
  beloved,
You and I
To the dream that we shall return
To our paradise

The one given to me when I had
  you
Where the winds of love were soft
  and playful
Exotic beneath exquisite trees
Where you, whom I loved so
  deeply,
Shall again caress my tired head.

Our last kiss was swift
Too swift, too short
As farewells slipped away
In the union of our lips
Quickly, with a smile
So very quickly.

My heart aches for you
As I must ask:
How will our final kiss
Survive eternity?

From the Holocaust library of Felix and Flory Van Beek.

Yom-Hashoah
IN MEMORIAM
OUR SIX MILLION MARTYRS

On Sunday night, May 27, 1945, the BBC broadcast an event from the concentration camp at Bergen-Belsen, Germany, where Dutch Jews had been transported during the Holocaust of 1940–1945. On this occasion, a number of Dutch Jewish children who had survived their ordeal in the camp sang a Dutch folk song in honor of their liberators, the American and British armed forces. The event was of such great emotional impact to the reporters and soldiers that one American Jewish officer tried to express his feelings by writing the attached poem, which was printed with great reverence in the Dutch newspapers in 1945. The last part of the poem contains the Jewish prayer of gratitude for life, in translation it means:

*"Blessed are Thou, O Lord, our God, King of the Universe who has kept us
in life, and has sustained us and enabled us to reach this season."*

THE SINGING CHILDREN OF BERGEN-BELSEN

A few meters away from the dead, the horror, the fierce stench which
    can never be forgotten by those who saw it,
     but will linger on forever,
And will bring fear to a soldier in the dark,
And will make him feel guilty should he once again be cheerful
Children are singing, innocent, as if they were celebrating a birthday,
They are singing in the camp of Bergen-Belsen
    for the soldiers who liberated them;
They sing a Dutch song, appropriate for the occasion:

*"May they live long, may they live long
Gloria, gloria"*

Is it not a contrast that they sing while their parents have been killed?
We hear their children's voices, so pure, so clear,
But before their eyes, innocent and unknowing,
    must be such dreadful visions
That even a knowing man's voice would stop

And yet, those children, who shared this horror for weeks, months, years,
How can they sing so unshaken,
These young orphans of Bergen-Belsen, standing there neatly,
    as if in a classroom, where someone just celebrated his birthday
Singing in just the right tune:

"May they live long, may they live long
Gloria, gloria"

Is it not strange that they should sing
With the little of what they remember from the past
Some songs perhaps, some memories,
Now, so hopelessly out of context
That it might be better to just forget;
Because, if death will shun away from them and if death
    will be their companion no longer,
Their lives will become very bitter in a world where
    they have no home, no parents
And everyone is left to strangers, to care for them
And yet: they are singing in their loving voices, so sweet and pure
As only a child's voice can be . . .

"May they live long, may they live long
Gloria, gloria"

While above the camp of Bergen-Belsen the sky is blue
And again, the larks fly jubilantly up to heaven
Because the summer is near,
The children acquire perhaps from their own singing a force,
Which ages could not break
A special force, which gave strength to generations before them,
    and which has kept them alive:
Now, to the voices of these innocent children of Bergen-Belsen
    so sweet and brave, I add my own voice
First, a bit husky and subdued, and hesitatingly . . .
But then I too sing . . . May they live long, may they live long . . .
Baruch Atah Adonay Eloheynu Melech Ha-Olam,
Shehecheyanu, Ve'kiyemanu, Ve'higiyanu Lazman Hazeh . . .

In Memoriam

Nel van der Veer-Brandsen, our beloved friend passed away September 4, 1998.